40 DAYS WITH THE HOLY SPIRIT

Chad Stafford

COPYRIGHT

40 Days with the Holy Spirit
Publisher: Team First Consulting & Media (May 8, 2021)
Language: English
ISBN-13: 9798736931354
Original Copyright © 2021 by Chad Stafford
Cover Design: Team First Consulting & Media
Editing and Format: Grace Lake Publishing
Printed in the United States of America.

DEDICATION

I dedicate this book to my son, Evan Charles Stafford, in whom I am well pleased.

Son, when we pass from this earth, our goal is to bless you with a good name, a godly example, and financial security. Most importantly, Mom and I have wanted to pass on an experience with God, as this was a game changer in our lives. God has given you a private prayer language where you can tap into his power anytime you need it. Your great-grandparents have experienced this gift, and they passed it to your grandparents, who passed it on to your mom and me. Now, it is your turn to share in this gift, and we praise God that you received some of your spiritual inheritance early in life. May the life-giving legacy of the Baptism of the Holy Spirit burn in you. May you take the responsibility to pour it into others. And may it spread through you to your generation.

You are everything I have ever wanted in a son and more.

I love you,

Dad

I.

PART ONE: THE STORY

CHAPTER 1

"If you roll your eyes at me one more time, I'm going to slug you!" Leo told Jake. They were less than twenty minutes into their journey.

Now that Leo's family had converted to the Jewish faith, a friendship with Jake may not have been optional, but he refused to listen to Jake's condescending tone and planned to remedy that right away. They were going to be stuck together for the next two weeks and the ground rules needed to be set now.

Both of the young men were thirteen years old yet could not have been more opposite from each other.

Jake was small and brainy, the star pupil of his father's class. He was named after his Jewish forefather, Jacob, whose name was later changed to "Israel" by an angel he'd wrestled with for an entire night.

Learning came easy to Jake. He connected with people intellectually long before he allowed them into his heart. He loved to teach and could explain every intricate detail of any subject that he discussed. He had memorized all of the Scriptures, and he immersed himself into his rabbinical studies. Everyone in his family said that Jake would not only follow in his father's footsteps as a rabbi, but, because of his instant grasp of the Torah, would surpass him.

Jake was wise beyond his years, an obedient rule follower,

and lived to study. He rarely spoke to boys his own age because he really could not relate to them. He preferred the company of older men, where he could sit and listen, ask questions, and learn.

Leo was five months older than Jake, a fact that he never let Jake forget. Leo grew up husky but had grown eight inches in the last six months and was starting to show some definition in his arms and stomach where there had previously been baby fat. Leo was aggressive, and puberty only seemed to add fuel to an already raging fire. Leo's recent growth spurt had made him clumsy. His father, Magnus, regularly teased him by saying that the first thing Leo did every morning after getting out of bed was stumble. Every time that his dad chuckled at his clumsiness, Leo took it as a personal invitation to wrestle. Leo even managed to pin him a few times because his dad could hardly catch his breath from the laughter.

Leo's ancestors were Greek. They were from the region of Sparta, known for its legendary armies. Leo was named after the great Spartan King Leonidas I, who led allied forces to a last stand at the Battle of Thermopylae with only 300 men. Although his family had been out of that region for over 200 years, Leo told everyone the origin of his name and did everything he could to resurrect his Spartan roots.

Although he was educated, Leo was also a man of action, and so he was bored by school. His teacher recently informed him that he had completed his education, and now he needed to begin to apprentice his trade. Upon hearing the news, Leo embraced his teacher and swung the little man around in circles. In his eyes, the teacher had given him the greatest gift of his life; unbeknownst to Leo, his teacher felt the same way.

Their parents brought these two young men together. Jake's dad, Isaac, was the town rabbi. Rabbi Isaac was brilliant, but instead of showing off his advanced learning, he made everyone in his presence feel smart. His teaching style on the Sabbath was masterful. He saw it as his job to make what was ordinarily complicated, simple.

Rabbi Isaac had an irresistible personality with a resounding laugh that everyone recognized. He loved being around people and it showed. Rabbi Isaac spoke to both Jews and Gentiles with the same charm and affection. Reaching out to his entire community, he witnessed many Gentile conversions. Three months ago, Leo's dad became one of them.

Magnus was a Roman army captain. As a centurion, he led nearly 100 soldiers. Magnus was large in frame and quickly advanced up the ranks by proving to be a very observant man. He was not reactionary like other soldiers. He was disciplined, methodical, and calm.

After leaving Sparta, Magnus' family embraced the Greeks' Stoic philosophy and held to this belief when they relocated to Rome 100 years before Magnus was born. Stoics were known for their wisdom, morality, courage, and moderation. These virtues produced great officers.

Magnus' unit was dispatched to the town four years earlier by the governor, and shortly after arriving, he became fascinated by the town rabbi who gladly spoke to everyone. On his previous assignments, town rabbis would have nothing to do with anyone who wasn't Jewish, but this town rabbi seemed to be genuinely interested in others.

While walking home one afternoon, Magnus was amazed when Rabbi Isaac introduced himself and respectfully asked,

"Officer, may I ask your name?"

Magnus' position and authority usually intimidated anyone who came in his path, so the question's cheerful tone shocked him. He answered, "My name is Magnus. Why do you ask?"

Rabbi Isaac smiled and answered him. "Every morning before the sun rises, I like to pray for the people who live in our town. With your permission, I would like to add your name. I will ask my God to bless and protect you and your family."

Magnus prayed to many gods so he figured one more couldn't hurt. Typically, he would have just walked away. But he had been observing Rabbi Isaac's cheerfulness for weeks, so he obliged his request with, "Sure, Rabbi. You go ahead and pray all you want."

Rabbi Isaac thanked him for the opportunity, and then he did the unthinkable. He bowed his head in honor and welcomed the officer to their town.

In shock at this gesture, Magnus' face broke his usual emotionless demeanor; he was glad the rabbi's head was bowed so he did not see his break in discipline. Magnus silently walked away in bewilderment. Later on, after the evening meal, he could not help but wonder why a man whose town was taken over by foreigners, would not only want to pray for him but welcome him there.

In the days following, Rabbi Isaac would further engage Magnus and ask where he was from and what he thought of the town. Magnus usually gave him short answers, trying to avoid much dialogue.

Over the next year, Magnus became less and less suspicious of the rabbi's intentions, as Rabbi Isaac's kind nature seemed consistent with everyone he encountered. Rich, poor, common, or powerful—this man was genuinely interested in the lives of others. He was a man of honor, and that was dependable.

Their conversations grew, and Magnus found himself asking questions about Judaism. The rabbi answered him with logical reasoning, yet, at the same time, there was something supernatural in his answers. What resonated with Magnus was that the rabbi's logical beliefs also dictated his lifestyle. To the Stoics, it was necessary for actions to follow your beliefs. Magnus concluded that it was more than just belief for the rabbi and his family; this was who they were at the core.

As Magnus began to seek to become a Gentile convert, he saw another side of the jovial rabbi. If becoming a Jew is what Magnus sought, he would have to study. He would study the Torah, take a written test, and then take a verbal test. Upon passing those steps, he would submit to an interview by the synagogue council of elders. Magnus was ready for the challenge.

Leo converted to Judaism as well, simply because his father did. In his culture, if dad converted, so did the entire family. Magnus would meet regularly with the rabbi continuing to learn in a one-on-one setting. But for Leo, the rabbi and the centurion had a rather unorthodox plan.

CHAPTER 2

"Are you kidding me? This is a joke, right?"

Leo could not believe that his father was serious when he announced they would be going with Rabbi Isaac and Jake to Jerusalem for a religious celebration. Magnus had regularly teased Leo about his "friendship" with Jake.

After their first encounter, Leo told his dad, "He is just the worst. I mean, it is one thing to be smart, but why do you have to try and prove it to the whole world?"

Magnus chuckled and replied, "You two are going to become the best of friends!"

As a result, after every Sabbath and any other occasion where the families were together, Magnus would grin and ask Leo, "How's your new best friend doing?" Leo would just roll his eyes and repeat his original answer firmly: "He's the worst."

With his gentle and wise countenance that Leo respected and longed to develop in himself, Magnus said, "No, son, I am serious. You and I will journey with our friends to Jerusalem to worship our God, Jehovah. We will continue to do this annually as a family. Your mother and sisters will stay behind this year because she is still recovering from your sister's birth and a two-day journey will be too much for her. However, as the men of this family, we will go together, learn more, and, when we return, we can prepare the family for the trip next year."

Leo adored his father, so he took a deep breath and submitted to the plan. As they packed for the trip, Magnus also relayed a new piece of information that Leo would like even less. While they traveled to the city, the boys would walk behind the men, and Jake, the future rabbi, would teach Leo what to expect at the feast.

Leo understood that his father was serious about his new faith and knew better than to argue with him about the arrangement. His father was a benevolent man, but when he presented a plan, his mind was made up, and he expected the soldiers under his charge, as well as his son, to execute that plan with absolute precision. His father's expectations were high, and everyone under his care would rather die than disappoint him.

As his father finished explaining, Leo obediently nodded. The centurion had spoken.

CHAPTER 3

When Rabbi Isaac told Jake that he had been tasked with teaching Leo, Jake was, as always, eager to share the content but had serious reservations about the student.

He found Leo to be rather brutish with seemingly no desire to grow in wisdom. Leo lived up to every stereotype Jake had heard about Greco-Roman soldiers. Leo was quick-tempered, combative, and aggressive, which Jake considered the deep character flaw of his culture.

Leo made him feel unsettled and nervous. After every conversation they had, Jake's stomach would ache. The less he had to be around Leo, the happier both of them would be, he thought.

"Father, as eager as I am to teach the Scriptures, I am convinced that there is not a rabbi alive who could teach a person like Leo," Jake said. "He is boorish and ignorant. He should follow in his father's footsteps and become a soldier. He could never be a student."

Rabbi Isaac had observed many of the same characteristics in Leo and knew them to be true. But, where Jake saw brutality, Rabbi Isaac saw energy. Where Jake saw apathy, Rabbi Isaac saw hunger. When Jake said, "He could never be a student," it cut Rabbi Isaac to the core.

Rabbi Isaac had long taught all of his students that anyone could be a student of the Scriptures. He repeated the phrase daily: "Anyone and everyone can be a student of God's Word." Although very few rabbis taught this, it was a steadfast belief of Rabbi Isaac's, and to know that his son disagreed made him feel like a failure as both a teacher and a father.

Jake saw the hurt in his father's eyes after his remarks. He loved his father deeply and his admiration for him knew no bounds, but he didn't retract what he said. Although it was an impulsive statement, Jake did not believe that just anyone could be a student of the Scriptures.

When God allowed him to become a rabbi, he would not teach that philosophy. Jake saw reaching out to the Gentiles as a waste of time. He would be different from his father when he was a rabbi. He would invest his time and energy exclusively in his own people. This is where his understanding of ministry and his father's idealistic worldview would separate.

Rabbi Isaac, with a disappointed smile, said to his prized pupil, "My son, there are no bad students; there are only bad teachers. Your first student may very well be your most difficult one, but the experience will shape the rest of your life."

Then, with a look of deep concern, he added, "You see, a rabbi's job is more than just knowing the information; it is about our belief in the students God sends to us. If the teacher does not believe in the student, the student cannot believe in himself. If you fail to understand this, you will fail the student and yourself."

Then the chubby rabbi smiled again, kissed the top of his son's head and said with a wink, "Goodnight, my son. Sleep well. We leave at first light for The City of the Great King."

For the first time in his life, Jake felt the full pressure of being a rabbi. He could scarcely remember a night when he slept less.

CHAPTER 4

"Why must you always respond with threats of violence?" Jake asked Leo. "The sun is barely up, we have a two-day journey together, and you are already bullying me."

The roosters had barely stopped crowing, and that nauseating feeling in Jake's stomach was already setting in.

Leo stopped walking and glared at Jake. "I'm not looking forward to this any more than you. You don't like me, and I don't like you, but the way that you talk to me is going to change or you are going to lose some teeth. I am older than you. You are not my teacher, and you certainly aren't my friend. But I told my dad that I would listen to what you had to say, and if you value your life, you are going to change the way that you say it."

Jake had never been told that someone wasn't his friend. At school, everyone had always wanted to be his friend. He was smart, capable, and admired. He always gave the correct answer and flourished in a classroom setting. He had never been in a fight and rarely ever raised his voice.

Jake couldn't admit it yet, but, as strong as his intellect was, people had always been a mystery to him. He was not shy, but he was not a fan of small talk. He did not engage in many social activities and didn't introduce himself to strangers the way his father did. He would chuckle to himself when he saw his dad do that, wondering why in the world he bothered.

Jake treasured his solitude. His favorite part of being the rabbi's son was the access he had to the temple. He could be in the temple as much as he wished, reading the Torah scrolls and writing down the Scriptures. There was a deep well inside of him that longed for the things of God. He would study late into the night and would feel the Spirit of God reverberating through the text.

Studying would be his lifelong pursuit, but he also loved listening to the men in the temple courts discuss the Scriptures. He had sat with them since he began school as a five-year-old boy. He got a free pass early on because he was the rabbi's son, but he instinctively knew how to sit and listen respectfully. Only after he began his rabbinical studies did he contribute to the discussion, and, on the few occasions when he did, it was poignant, humble, and wise. The elders knew that he was someone special.

Somehow, that "special-ness" was lost when he was around Leo.

Leo was not going to let anyone look down on him or treat him in a condescending manner. Especially some little Jewish kid who thought he was "God's gift" to the world.

If they were going to have to be stuck together, Leo wanted to engage in the conversation. Leo wanted to have a dialogue, while Jake wanted to give a monologue.

Leo had asked a question earlier, and as Jake answered it, he rolled his eyes at him. Leo let that one slide, thinking it better to let their fathers get a little farther ahead beyond earshot. The second time Leo asked a question, he was more strategic. The older men were chatting about 100 yards ahead, and that's when Leo set Jake straight.

Out of sheer intimidation, Jake apologized. "I'm sorry. I barely slept last night, and my stomach is hurting," Jake said.

"Keep it up, and there's going to be more than your stomach that's going to hurting," Leo threatened.

When he saw the fear in Jake's eyes, he relented and began walking. The older men had not seen them stop, but he didn't want to chance it so early in the day.

CHAPTER 5

They walked in silence for hours. Jake was content to not speak again until their dads forced them to. After about four hours, Leo needed the distraction. "So, yeah, what's the name of this celebration again?" he asked Jake.

Jake focused himself on making sure that he did not answer derogatorily and replied, "It's called the Feast of Pentecost. It's the harvest festival of the Jewish people. Sometimes, it's referred to as the Festival of Weeks."

Leo nodded and asked, "And why do you guys have to go?"

This question was going to be Jake's sweet spot. This is where he thrived. He was going to quote the Scripture and show off his knowledge to Leo.

"Moses required the nation of Israel to do so. In Exodus 34:22, he wrote, 'Celebrate the Festival of Weeks with the firstfruits of the wheat harvest, and the Festival of Ingathering at the turn of the year.'

"He said it again in Numbers 28:26: 'On the day of firstfruits, when you present to the Lord an offering of new grain during the Festival of Weeks, hold a sacred assembly and do no regular work.'

"He said it twice in the sixteenth chapter of Deuteronomy. First in verse 10: 'Then celebrate the Festival of Weeks to the Lord your God by giving a freewill offering in proportion to the blessings the Lord your God has given you.' And, again in verse 16: 'Three times a year, all your men must appear before the Lord your God at the place he will choose: at the Festival of Unleavened Bread, the Festival of Weeks and the Festival of Tabernacles. No one should appear before the Lord empty-handed.'"

Very proud of his recall, Jake added, "The Feast of Unleavened Bread is the Feast of Passover, which we celebrated a few weeks ago. There are seven weeks between Passover and Pentecost. Pentecost means 'fiftieth.' First comes Passover, and Pentecost is fifty days later."

Leo, surprisingly impressed with Jake, replied, "I hope this feast is better than the Passover one. That one was kind of dreary."

Jake could not hide his laughter because it was the first time that he and Leo had ever agreed on anything. "Passover is very sad and serious. But Passover is a joyous occasion, too. In fact, all the festivals are. Only Yom Kippur is somber, and it is a fast, not a feast. Passover, though, is the Jewish celebration of freedom. But Pentecost is anything but boring. It is fun! There is music and food and dancing. It's nothing like Passover."

Leo was relieved at this and smiled. So far, he had not been looking forward to it, but now he thought it might not be so bad.

He then asked, "How do you guys do it all? I mean, don't you have to work?"

Jake answered, "Oh, no. During the holy days, we are off from work."

Leo shook his head. "That is cool but so weird to me. I mean, if Dad says we are Jewish now, I am fine with that. Before Dad joined up with you guys, he never had a day off from work. Now, he doesn't work on Saturdays and he gets off for stuff like this, too."

Jake had never heard it from this perspective before. The more they talked, the bigger both of their worlds became.

Jake jumped on the opportunity here to teach a little more and said, "The Sabbath was always part of our culture. We believe that we don't keep the Sabbath as much as the Sabbath keeps us. God shows us in the fourth commandment that the Sabbath started in Creation. And when God established it this way in Creation, it is a picture of what God wants to give us."

Leo, actually enjoying what Jake was saying, asked, "What kind of picture do you think your God wants to show you guys?"

Jake answered enthusiastically, "You see, all of the other cultures, just like yours, work seven days a week. The Sabbath was just another day to them, but God wants the Jewish people to stand out so that people like you who were not born Jewish would ask me a question about why we take a day off."

Leo jumped in and said, "I once remember a merchant asking a Jewish man in the town square, 'How can your people do more work in less time than us? How can you make more money than us by taking a day off? That doesn't make sense!'"

Jake, feeling a connection with Leo for the first time, laughed and said, "Yes! God wanted a day off to be a blessing so much that he made it into a law. When God commanded the Jewish people at Sinai to take a day off, God was telling them, 'I want you to trust me, that I will bless you with more than enough. I want you to rest and be refreshed!' And God does this because he wants to provide for us supernaturally."

Leo, still in awe of what he was learning, said, "It doesn't make sense, but I can tell you over the last several months since my dad joined the temple, he seems different. He seems happier and more at peace. Are you telling me that is because he takes a day off?"

"No, Leo, it is so much bigger than that. After God made us take off on Saturdays, God spoke to Moses and told the people that, not only were they to take a day off every week, but every seventh year they were not to plant any crops. He told them to let the land rest. He promised to bless his people so much in the sixth year that they would have more than enough. He promised to take care of us if we would only trust him."

"What?" Leo said. "That is crazy! I almost wish I was a farmer's kid now instead of a centurion's kid. No matter how good of a leader my dad is, somehow I don't think Emperor Tiberius would allow a year off."

Jake was laughing so hard now that both Rabbi Isaac and Magnus turned around to see what the commotion was about.

At first, Magnus thought the noise he heard was Jake crying for help and that he was going to have to pull Leo off of him.

Instinct pulled Magnus toward the boys, but Rabbi Isaac grabbed his arm and said, "No, wait. I think they are laughing."

They watched them for a moment and looked at each other in disbelief. Rabbi Isaac rarely saw his son laugh like that.

"I'm pretty sure that I have just witnessed my first miracle," Magnus said.

Rabbi Isaac shook his head. "My brother, I would have to agree."

After Jake composed himself, he shared the teachings that his father always gave regarding the Sabbath. No one was better at bringing application to the text than Rabbi Isaac.

In the kind tone and gentle cadence of his father, he asked, "Now Leo, if God cares this much about a day of the week, and if he cares this much about our land, how much more so does he care about us?"

Sixty years later, as an old man, Jake would tell his great-grandson that this was the moment he became a rabbi.

CHAPTER 6

For the rest of the afternoon, Leo asked more questions and Jake taught him with great enthusiasm. He was impressed with Leo's hunger to learn and the ease with which he listened.

Leo wasn't as skeptical as many of the students at Jake's school, and it was so refreshing to see someone quickly grasp the principles of God's Word.

Leo's humility was having a significant impact on Jake. Jake wanted to speak gently and kind to him as he answered his questions. Where once he had only seen typical pagan aggression, he now saw someone who was made in God's image.

Leo was not fortunate enough to be raised in the faith like he had been, and now Jake saw it as his responsibility to honor the Torah with how he spoke to him. Leo was new to their country and their way of thinking. How Jake had been speaking to Leo in the previous months was sinful. God commanded the nation of Israel to be hospitable to outsiders all throughout the Scriptures. God commanded Israel to be kind to aliens and strangers because their future would be dependent upon them.

All of the Scriptures that Jake had long since memorized began flooding his mind and reminding him of his sin. From the Pentateuch to the writings of the prophets, the double-edged sword of God's Word penetrated his heart.

God told his people in Exodus 23:9: "Do not oppress a foreigner; you yourselves know how it feels to be foreigners, because you were foreigners in Egypt."

By acting superior and speaking condescendingly to Leo, Jake was oppressing him by making him feel inferior. God expected more out of his people when it came to how they treated outsiders.

God wanted Israel to be generous with their kindness, with their time, and with their blessings. He even told them in the book of Leviticus: "When you reap the harvest of your land, do not reap to the very edges of your field or gather the gleanings of your harvest. Do not go over your vineyard a second time or pick up the grapes that have fallen. Leave them for the poor and the foreigner. I am the Lord your God." (Leviticus 19:9-10)

God wanted his people to be kind, generous, and patient with others, and Jake had been anything but that with Leo. It was now becoming clear to Jake that God cared as much for Leo as he did for him. After all, God had said later in Leviticus 24:22: "You are to have the same law for the foreigner and the native-born. I am the Lord your God."

Jake spoke differently to Leo than he did to Jewish kids. He didn't see Leo as equal to him. He had considered Leo beneath him. Not only did Jake know the Scriptures didn't teach that, but Rabbi Isaac modeled a better way for him, and he had refused to follow it. Jake knew better and had seen better but refused to obey. His brain raced forward to Deuteronomy 10:19: "And you are to love those who are foreigners, for you yourselves were foreigners in Egypt."

It was then that Jake realized that he was prejudiced. Leo

was outside of his ethnicity and Jake was uncomfortable with that. He had seen non-Jews as inferior, and his attitude up to this point had reflected that.

Jake knew God's Word, saw the right example in his father, and still knowingly broke God's law. Jake was a sinner, and like the generations before him, he was breaking God's heart with how he treated others. He had felt that he was so good in the eyes of God for so long. Now, he realized that was simply not the case.

Jake began to feel sick to his stomach again and started to sweat.

"Hey man, are you alright?" Leo asked. "You are awfully pale. Are you getting too hot?"

Up until that point, Leo had been talking about some war that his grandfather had fought in, but Jake had tuned him out and had been listening inwardly. He knew what he had to do.

Every year since he was five years old, Jake traveled to Jerusalem with his father for the Festival of Yom Kippur to confess his sins and offer up the sacrifice for his forgiveness. But Jake also knew that before a man could ask forgiveness from God, he must ask forgiveness from others.

On the verge of tears, Jake put his head down to hide his face. "Leo, I need to say something. I don't mean to interrupt, but would you mind?" Jake asked.

Leo was somewhat confused by the courtesy. He was used to Jake's mannerisms and had never seen this side of him. This seemed more like Rabbi Isaac, not Jake. Whatever Jake wanted to say must have been important.

Jake normally avoided eye contact with Leo, but now he was standing face to face in full attention, so Leo replied, "Uh … yeah. Sure. Go ahead."

Jake swallowed hard. "Leo, I am sorry for how I have treated you since we first met. My attitude was wrong. The things that I have said about you were wrong. I know better. I need to apologize to you and ask for your forgiveness." When he finished his confession, it was as if someone had poured cool water on him and he felt relief.

Leo stared at him inquisitively and with as much sensitivity as he could muster said, "Yeah. Okay. Just don't puke on me, alright? Geez."

Jake breathed a loud sigh of relief. "Thank you, Leo."

Leo, now completely weirded out but also in awe of the change in Jake's tone and attitude, rolled his eyes and said, "No problem."

They continued walking on for a little while in awkward silence, but with it came something new—mutual respect.

CHAPTER 7

That evening as they finished their dinner and sat around the fire, Jake looked forward to catching up on some of the sleep that he missed the previous night. His body was tired, but his heart was full. The joy of teaching God's Word and the amazement of seeing someone through new eyes created a fulfillment inside of him that he didn't know could exist.

Jake had never laughed more in his life, and on that long journey he had discovered that, beyond the aggression and the machismo, there was a depth to Leo. Leo was sincere in his curiosity of this newfound faith of his family. The confidence that Leo had in Magnus and of his leadership was genuine and refreshing.

Leo would ask a question and once Jake explained it, that was enough for him. There wasn't much debate at all. Leo didn't have all of the answers, and he didn't seem to need them. Leo was older than Jake, but he still possessed a child-like trust that fascinated Jake.

Leo made teaching easy and didn't need for someone to overexplain it to him. He couldn't wait to discuss the teachings again the next day. Even though his body was worn out, his mind raced with anticipation. It took some time for him to relax enough to fall asleep, but once he did, he slept soundly.

They were once again up at daylight the following morning, and as the sun shone brighter, Jake whispered his prayer of thanksgiving for the day, The Shema:

"Hear, O Israel: The Lord our God, the Lord is one. Love the Lord your God with all your heart and with all your soul and with all your strength. These commandments that I give you today are to be on your hearts. Impress them on your children. Talk about them when you sit at home and when you walk along the road, when you lie down and when you get up. Tie them as symbols on your hands and bind them on your foreheads. Write them on the doorframes of your houses and on your gates." (Deuteronomy 6:4-5, Deuteronomy 11:13-21, Numbers 15:37-41)

He had recited that prayer every day for the past eight years out of ritual and duty, but, today, he said it with joy and peace as he never had before.

CHAPTER 8

There was a different atmosphere surrounding the boys as they walked together this morning. There was an eagerness to both teach and listen. The two fathers were in awe of how their worlds had changed in the past twenty-four hours.

"So, what all should I expect here?" Leo asked excitedly.

"A lot of fun! There will be music, singing, and dancing," Jake said.

"Since it's a celebration of the harvest, I can imagine there will be a lot of good food, and I can't wait to try it all!" Leo said. After his recent growth spurt, it seemed like he was always hungry.

Jake just grinned. "Correct! You are catching on quickly."

Leo laughed. "I am all ears when it comes to food. Plus, you explain things pretty well. It makes me want to know more."

"Wow. Thanks for saying that. It's pretty much a nonstop party, and then right near the end, there are some things that you will want to be familiar with so that you can understand the symbolism," Jake explained. "There will be a ceremony where the high priest will come and begin waving the loaves of bread. It's called a peace offering, and it symbolizes eating a meal with God, which is what most of the festival is about."

Leo nodded. "And that's the end of it?"

"No, that's not it. Before we leave, the high priest reads the account of Mt. Sinai," Jake answered.

"What happened there?" Leo asked.

Jake was more reflective now and his tone more somber. "Yeah. We basically blew it as a people at Mt. Sinai. God gave Moses the Ten Commandments on top of Mt. Sinai, and when he came down to give it to us ... well ... let me start from the beginning."

"Leo," Jake continued, "The setting was amazing. Not one person was missing. Everyone was gathered together. God was committing to us and we were going to commit to him, similar to a wedding. Israel was going to return back to God and agree to be his flesh and blood representatives to the world. The ancient rabbis wrote that at Sinai the whole world was silent, not even a bird chirped because everyone everywhere heard the voice of God calling humanity into a relationship with its Creator."

"That sounds awesome," Leo said, trying to imagine the scene.

"Oh, there's more, Leo. Those same ancient rabbis wrote that at Mt. Sinai tongues of fire went out to all the nations so that all people everywhere could hear God's voice in a language that they could understand."

"This may be the coolest thing that I have ever heard!" Leo said, flabbergasted. "Tongues of fire? Just picturing that in my head seems incredible. I'm kind of a pyromaniac; I love fire!"

Jake smiled and continued, "In the Scriptures, fire is mentioned when the outpouring of God's Spirit happens. It happened to the prophets Isaiah, Ezekiel, Joel, and Zechariah. It symbolizes fiery speech. And one time, the prophet Elijah challenged the prophets of Baal on Mt. Carmel to a showdown. The prophets of Baal prepared a sacrifice to their false god and prayed all day for him to answer, but their god never did. But when Elijah prepared his sacrifice, he poured four huge pots of water all over it three different times to make it seem harder for God to answer. But when Elijah prayed, God not only burned up the sacrifice, but a tongue of fire licked up the water!"

Leo's mouth dropped wide open. He was now transfixed with the stories of his new faith. He could not wait to tell his younger siblings what he had learned. "I just don't know what to say. I can't decide whether to be amazed or afraid."

Jake chuckled and said, "Congratulations. You are now a Jew, Leo! Because that might be the most Jewish thing that I have ever heard you say."

Leo, now chuckling too, replied, "Why do you say that?"

Jake stopped walking and looked at his new friend. "Because, at Sinai, we didn't know whether to be amazed or scared either."

Jake continued with a melancholy look and tone. "Jake, we broke our deal with God before the ink was dry on the contract. By the end of the day, God had to kill 3,000 of us. So, needless to say, our memories of all of us being together in one place at one time is not a very good one."

Leo let the moment sink in for a few seconds, squinted his eyes in deep thought, and said, "So, let me get this straight.

Before you can leave the festival, you have to take time to remember how you blew it with God at Sinai? That's kind of depressing after all that fun."

Jake nodded his head in agreement and added, "I see where you can think that. We use this time to reflect and remember that in spite of all of our failures, God still blesses us; he lets our crops grow, gives our bodies time to rest and recover. With all of this goodness, it seems like all we can do is break our commitments to him. But Pentecost reminds us that one day all of our failures and the way that we disappointed God won't be a constant reminder because God will once again pour out his power on us. This time, God won't be living in a tabernacle, or on top of Mt. Sinai, or putting his power on stone tablets. The next time he pours out his Spirit, he will begin living inside of his people. That fire that you love so much, Leo. It's not just a symbol of God's power and his presence, but it's also a symbol of God's acceptance. One day, his people won't just be people who find new ways to disappoint him anymore because God will be living inside of us. We will be pure and spotless because God has accepted us as his own."

Quietly and slowly, Leo said, "Whoa, man. That is heavy." Then, he snapped back to reality. "Jews have a symbol for everything, don't we?"

Jake smiled, shaking his head. "Yep. But when you know the symbols, it creates a picture of God that is unforgettable."

"It definitely does, my friend," Leo said.

Jake smiled and took in the moment. It was the first time Leo called him "friend."

CHAPTER 9

The boys enjoyed the rest of their day. They made camp about two hours outside of Jerusalem. With any luck, they would arrive at the festival at about eight o'clock the next morning.

"Before we go to sleep, I'd like to share something with all of you," Rabbi Isaac said.

"Over the last three years, we have all heard of the incredible teacher at the temple named Jesus. His popularity is known all over Israel. He came to our village, and he healed the sick, the blind, and the lame. Our people loved him. Jake and I have also heard him teach a few times on trips into Jerusalem, and he was amazing. I am quite sure that he was the Messiah that God has promised us."

Rabbi Isaac continued, "His love and care for people and his profound understanding of Scripture, no one could dispute. His commitment to God and the purity with which he carried himself challenged our leaders in ways that made them feel very uncomfortable. Jesus could not be bought, manipulated, or forced to do anything even slightly unethical. He loved the rich and the poor. He exposed our leader's hypocrisy, and, a few weeks ago, during Passover, they crucified him for it. The temple leaders planned it out methodically and executed their plan during the most popular time of the festival. They beat him privately all through the night. They had him flogged in the morning, and in an effort to intimidate any of his present or future followers, they forced him to carry his own cross through the streets when they were the most crowded. He died at exactly three o'clock in the afternoon when the Passover lambs are sacrificed, and when he did, the temple veil was torn in two."

"Rabbi, why was there a veil at the temple?" Leo asked.

"That's a great question, Leo," Rabbi Isaac said. "At the temple, there is a curtain that separates all of the people from the presence of God. The high priest can only enter it once a year to offer the sacrifice for the sins of the nation. Many now believe that Jesus was the lamb of God that was slain for all of our sins. It appears that because of Jesus' death on the cross, we now have no barriers between us and God. The sacrifice has been paid in full."

"Outstanding!" Magnus exclaimed.

"And not only that, Jesus is said to have risen from the dead and has appeared to nearly 500 people on ten different occasions over the last forty days. His students said that he ascended into heaven a few days ago at Bethany."

"That is unheard of—a man who defeated death!" Leo said, shaking his head in amazement.

Rabbi Isaac continued, "And before he ascended into heaven, Jesus told everyone not to leave Jerusalem until they received a gift that he promised them. He said they were going to be immersed and filled with the power of the Holy Spirit. Something tells me that this particular feast is going to be very special."

Rabbi Isaac squinted his eyes in a contemplative manner as if he were trying to solve a great mystery. "It would make perfect sense for this infilling of the Spirit of God to take place at the Feast of Pentecost. We reflect upon God pouring out his power at the end of every feast, and we dream about the day when God will do this. Not only that, but it is a required feast, so every Jew in the known world will be there."

He concluded his predictions with the same peaceful smile that his community loved. "Everything our God does is for a reason and happens at the perfect time. I am anxiously anticipating what God might do. I now hope that you are too."

"Who can sleep after hearing something as amazing as that?" Magnus said.

"Amen, brother," Rabbi Isaac said.

"Amen, sir," said Jake.

Everyone looked at Leo and waited.

"Oh. I'm sorry. Uh ... Amen, Dad," Leo said as they all laughed together.

Morning couldn't come soon enough.

CHAPTER 10

All of the men kept waking up throughout the night hoping that sunrise was near. They were so eager to begin their journey and wondered if daylight would ever come.

Rabbi Isaac was the first to get up and began to stoke the remaining embers of the fire, which seemed to give everyone else permission to rise as well. The moon was bright, but they were so excited that they left an hour before the sun rose.

Jerusalem, it seemed, had not slept at all. They could hear the music from two miles outside the city, and it grew louder and louder as they walked toward the temple. When the men arrived inside the city gates, people were eating their breakfasts and already singing.

Leo thought that Jake totally undersold the celebration of the Feast of Pentecost. The joy, the dancing, and the atmosphere of the festival could not be adequately described with words. It had to experienced.

Everything around was so inspirational that it engaged every sense. It was impossible to count the number of smiles on all of the faces. This little nation that started with one man named Abraham had risen from nothing to world prominence because of the blessings of God. It was a family reunion.

Vast crowds were already gathered in the streets. As they

made their way through, Leo accidentally stepped on the foot of an older gentleman in front of him.

When the man turned around, Leo immediately apologized. "I'm so sorry, sir. I didn't mean to."

The older man smiled from ear to ear, let out a booming laugh, and yelled, "You are fine, my brother!" The man put his arm around Leo and squeezed his shoulder like a proud grandfather, then turned and danced away into the streets.

Leo's mouth was agape with shock. The only man who had ever shown such affection to Leo was his father, so this inter-action was genuinely awkward for him. As Leo turned back to look at his traveling companions, they were laughing hys-terically. Leo found himself starting to feel embarrassed and Jake compassionately stepped in to comfort his new friend.

"Don't worry, Leo," said Jake. "I was around five years old when a stranger at Pentecost picked me up and swung me around as he danced. It scared me so much that I began to cry."

Rabbi Isaac grinned and helped to further ease the tension when he added, "And if I recall, son, your face wasn't the only thing that was wet after that encounter."

Jake smiled and let out a shy laugh. "I was hoping you forgot that part."

"So, it scared you so bad you peed on yourself?" Leo asked, finally beginning to smile again.

Jake just smiled, closed his eyes, and nodded embarrassingly.

Rabbi Isaac then declared, "You have now officially arrived at the Feast of Pentecost, Leo!"

Leo looked up at his dad to see him smiling in a way that he only saw when he was around his family. Pentecost was becoming for Leo a bonding experience that he longed for in the deep places of his soul he didn't even know existed.

As they continued to walk, the music was so loud that the men had to shout to hear one another.

Magnus smelled the bread from a nearby booth and remarked to the guys, "That bread smells wonderful." And just as the words came out of his mouth, the music stopped abruptly causing his voice to be amplified.

"Well, have some, then!" a smiling lady told him and ran to them with four rolls. Before he could object, the warm bread was already in their hands. The sweet lady waited for him to take a bite and, as he did, it melted in his mouth.

Magnus reached for his money and was going to happily pay for the most wonderful bread he had ever eaten, when Rabbi Isaac stopped him and shook his head no.

Recognizing that he was unfamiliar with their custom, the hospitable lady asked, "Sir, forgive me for asking, but is this your first time coming to the feast?"

"Yes, ma'am," Magnus answered bashfully.

The kind woman smiled and patted his hand. "Son, no one leaves Pentecost hungry," she said in a gentle and motherly tone, before disappearing back into the crowd.

Magnus swallowed hard and barely managed to hold back the tears. He had not been called "son" for nearly forty years. The last time he heard that word was the day his mother died. Pentecost made him feel at home and that he belonged to a family again—a family even bigger and more powerful than Rome. Magnus knew that he was truly among his people.

As they made their way toward the temple, they could hear the various languages of Jews from all over the world. Although the language was different, the smiles and atmosphere remained the same among them.

For the Jewish people, Pentecost was about being together in the same place, even though they may live far apart. Leo couldn't help but feel a sense of awe over how numerous and inclusive God's family truly is.

CHAPTER 11

As they walked closer to the temple, they took in everything about the feast. Magnus and Leo were mesmerized by all the sights and sounds. They felt so honored as Rabbi Isaac and Jake proudly introduced them as their "dear brothers" to some of their old friends and family. They all welcomed Magnus and Leo with open arms and made plans to meet up later during the festival for an evening meal. The men thanked them and told them how much they were looking forward to spending more time together.

About two blocks from the temple square, a crowd was gathering outside of a sprawling building with a beautiful upstairs terrace that overlooked the bustling crowds lining the streets.

As Rabbi Isaac, Magnus, Jake, and Leo walked toward the temple, a loud thunderclap came from above.

"Aww man, we were having such a good time and now a storm is coming," Leo said.

Magnus said, "It sounds like it's about to storm but there isn't a cloud in the sky. I wonder what that's all about?"

At this, Rabbi Isaac stopped walking and stood silently. The look on his face expressed to everyone the seriousness of the moment. Jake looked at his father and knew that something was out of the ordinary.

They stared at Rabbi Isaac, who closed his eyes and intently listened to the sound of the wind. After a few seconds, tears streamed down from his face and he whispered, "His name be praised."

While their eyes were transfixed on their leader, Rabbi Isaac dried the tears with his sleeves, then his chubby grin returned. "We need to get to the temple. Something is about to happen."

They were headed in the direction of the temple when Jake said, "The noise is coming from that house with the nice terrace. That must be why there is a crowd gathering."

They joined the crowd in the streets and looked up at the balcony where they saw men and women in deep prayer. The noise continued to grow around them and then someone said, "What is that dangling above their heads? Is that a torch of some kind?"

Leo elbowed Jake. "Is that what I think it is?"

With his eyes transfixed on the terrace, Jake slowly nodded his head yes. What began 1,300 years before, Jake knew he was witnessing come to fruition firsthand. What some had perceived as folklore passed down from older men, was a reality that was now happening right in front of him.

Leo whispered, "Tongues of fire, Jake. Just like at Mt. Sinai."

Jake nodded again, completely captivated by the sight.

A well-dressed young man who was standing beside them heard Leo and asked, "What is this? Why is there a tongue of fire hanging above them? I am a guest of a friend and from out of town."

Leo waited for Jake to say something, but Jake couldn't answer. So, Leo then began to teach the man what his friend taught him less than two days before.

"The ancient rabbis tell us that at Mt. Sinai when God brought the law to Israel, tongues of fire went out to all the nations so that all people everywhere could hear God's voice in a language they could understand. God is visiting his people now just like he did that day on the mountain."

Leo was impressed with his recall and Jake smiled and nodded approvingly at his student.

"That explains it," the man said. "You see, I am a Roman citizen from Crete. I work as a spice exporter. Because of my travels, I have been taught three different languages. My friend who invited me said that because of the crowds, I could sell a lot of my goods during Pentecost."

He continued and pointed to a man who appeared to be one of the leaders. "That man on the balcony is dressed like a Jewish fisherman from this region, but he is speaking Greek with a southern dialect that is distinctive to Crete. He doesn't look wealthy enough to travel or be educated. There is no way that he should know our language. His accent is flawless."

The Jewish fisherman on the balcony continued speaking in Greek and Jake asked the man from Crete what he was saying.

The young Cretan replied, "He said that God loves us and everything we see happening right now is because of his love for us. He said God wants to live inside of us and that we are now his temple. He wants to fill us with his presence like he filled the great temple on the day when Solomon dedicated it to him."

"Wow!" Leo and Jake said together. God was pouring out his Spirit right before their eyes. The crowd began to swell, and more of the visitors to Jerusalem were saying the same thing about these men and women speaking supernaturally in an unknown language.

There were so many questions from the growing crowd that the Jewish fisherman began to explain to the crowd what Jake and Leo already knew. God was pouring out his Spirit on his people and none of them would ever be the same again.

II.

PART TWO: THE STUDY

INTRODUCTION

The first section of this book is a fictional account designed to help you better understand Jewish imagery, as well as to put yourself in the context of understanding more clearly what the Day of Pentecost was like.

The second part of the book is where we will begin a 40-day journey together to learn more about the person of the Holy Spirit and to unlearn some of the stereotypes and bad teaching we may have heard.

Although I didn't discover this until after I finished writing the book, the number 40 in the Bible is always associated with cleansing and purifying.

For example, in the account of Noah and the ark, it rained 40 days and 40 nights when God sent the flood to destroy the wickedness on the earth.

Interestingly, Moses' life can be divided into three stages: 40 years in Egypt, 40 years in the desert, and a 40-year journey into the Promised Land. He also fasted 40 days twice.

God also sent Jonah to Nineveh and gave the people 40 days to repent. They did and God sent a revival there.

Elijah fasted for 40 days in the desert and, during that time, he received new direction from God. After that fast, his insecurities were broken, his doubts were removed, and he received a word that affected the next generation.

40 days is associated with spiritual cleansing and the purifying of our lives and bodies, which is what we need as we pursue a greater intimacy with the Holy Spirit.

Over the next 40 days, I want to encourage you to get to know the Holy Spirit and ask him to reveal himself to you in ways that you never imagined.

These daily devotionals will only take three to five minutes to read. You may be tempted to read on and finish it quickly, but I want to challenge you not to just skip ahead to hurry and finish. This isn't just a book to read, but a 40-day experience with the Holy Spirit. This is a journey that can begin to cultivate a deep lifelong relationship with the Holy Spirit. This is a daily appointment where our spirits grow and create a larger space for the Holy Spirit to occupy.

Read it. Take the time to absorb what it says. Study and examine it.

It's not enough just to know about the Holy Spirit. He wants to be experienced.

DAY 1

THE BAPTISM OF THE HOLY SPIRIT IN THE OLD TESTAMENT: PART 1

...till the Spirit is poured on us from on high, and the desert becomes a fertile field, and the fertile field seems like a forest. The Lord's justice will dwell in the desert, his righteousness live in the fertile field. The fruit of that righteousness will be peace; its effect will be quietness and confidence forever. My people will live in peaceful dwelling places, in secure homes, in undisturbed places of rest. (Isaiah 32:15-18)

As you may know, in studying theology, before we begin to adopt something as doctrine, there must first be what is called a "normative pattern" throughout Scripture. A normative pattern is clarified by it appearing in Scripture, in its context, at least five times. In the Old Testament alone, the Baptism of the Holy Spirit is mentioned twenty-four times, which leads us to our text today.

The author, the prophet Isaiah, is continuing with his theme of prophesying about the worldwide reign of Christ. He is telling his audience about the righteous life that Christ will live, and how his followers will also live in this righteousness and closely follow the teachings of God's Word.

He begins to talk about how the righteousness and blessings of God's people will be possible because God's Spirit will be poured out upon the people, and the Spirit will begin to work in their hearts. We know that this was made possible because of the death, burial, and resurrection of Jesus Christ.

On the Day of Pentecost, this prophecy was fulfilled when the Spirit of God was poured out on believers:

> But you will receive power when the Holy Spirit comes on you; and you will be my witnesses in Jerusalem, and in all Judea and Samaria, and to the ends of the earth. (Acts 1:8)

> All of them were filled with the Holy Spirit and began to speak in other tongues as the Spirit enabled them. (Acts 2:4)

God spoke of the Baptism of the Holy Spirit all throughout the Old Testament so that we could have a clear point of reference in which to begin our search, our experience, and ultimately our life.

DAY 2

THE BAPTISM OF THE HOLY SPIRIT IN THE OLD TESTAMENT: PART 2

For I will pour water on the thirsty land, and streams on the dry ground; I will pour out my Spirit on your offspring, and my blessing on your descendants. They will spring up like grass in a meadow, like poplar trees by flowing streams. Some will say, 'I belong to the Lord;' others will call themselves by the name of Jacob; still others will write on their hand, 'The Lord's,' and will take the name Israel. (Isaiah 44:3-5)

Today, as we continue our study of the Baptism of the Holy Spirit in the Old Testament, we will once again be in the book of Isaiah. One of the reasons for this is that the book of Isaiah has more revelation about God's nature, majesty, and holiness than any other book in the Old Testament.

In this particular passage, Isaiah is speaking, and what many may not understand is that his audience is, for the most part, totally backslidden. "Backslidden" means to have walked away or abandoned a relationship with God.

Isaiah tells the people that there will be a day when the Holy Spirit will be poured out on a future generation. This was partially fulfilled on the Day of Pentecost and will be totally fulfilled for Israel when they receive Christ as the Messiah:

In the last days, God says, I will pour out my Spirit on all people. Your sons and daughters will prophesy, your young men will see visions, your old men will dream dreams. Even on my servants, both men and women, I will pour out my Spirit in those days, and they will prophesy. (Acts 2:17-18)

I do not want you to be ignorant of this mystery, brothers and sisters, so that you may not be conceited: Israel has experienced a hardening in part until the full number of the Gentiles has come in, and in this way all Israel will be saved. As it is written: "The deliverer will come from Zion; he will turn godlessness away from Jacob." (Romans 11:25-26)

The outpouring of the Holy Spirit is always associated with restoration, blessing, and fruitfulness. It is what gives us the testimony we read about in our opening text when Isaiah writes, "I belong to the Lord." The Holy Spirit creates in us the confidence that we belong to God, that he is our Father, and that we have the rights and privileges of being his children.

Paul confirms this later on in the New Testament:

The Spirit himself testifies with our spirit that we are God's children. (Romans 8:16)

Because you are his sons, God sent the Spirit of his Son into our hearts, the Spirit who calls out, 'Abba, Father.' (Galatians 4:6)

We can thank God today that in spite of our past sins and our present shortcomings, his precious Holy Spirit constantly reminds us that we are his and he is ours. Hallelujah!

DAY 3

THE BAPTISM OF THE HOLY SPIRIT IN THE OLD TESTAMENT: PART 3

I will no longer hide my face from them, for I will pour out my Spirit on the people of Israel, declares the Sovereign Lord. (Ezekiel 39:29)

Much like Isaiah, the prophet Ezekiel was sent to speak to Israel when they were in a backslidden state. During his time, Ezekiel also emphasized the personal responsibility of each individual before God instead of just passing it off as the result of the sin of their ancestors.

In Chapters 4-32, Ezekiel speaks about the dark and gloomy judgment that God is going to pour out upon Israel. But, in Chapter 33, the text switches from judgment to comfort and the assurance of a future hope. He begins to speak of revival and a restoration that will come when God becomes their True Shepherd again.

In Ezekiel 36:26-27, God promises to give them a "new heart" and a "new spirit," and to place his Spirit in them as well. God tells Ezekiel that he will no longer hide his face from his people.

In other words, God is promising to speak to us like he spoke to Jesus—face to face. Not because of anything that we have done, but because we have been made worthy by the shed blood of Jesus Christ. We will be able to know God face to face because we have been made right with God. When we have a new spirit, God can pour into us new things.

DAY 4

THE BAPTISM OF THE HOLY SPIRIT IN THE OLD TESTAMENT: PART 4

And afterward, I will pour out my Spirit on all people. Your sons and daughters will prophesy, your old men will dream dreams, your young men will see visions. Even on my servants, both men and women, I will pour out my Spirit in those days. I will show wonders in the heavens and on the earth, blood and fire and billows of smoke. The sun will be turned to darkness and the moon to blood before the coming of the great and dreadful day of the Lord. And everyone who calls on the name of the Lord will be saved; for on Mount Zion and in Jerusalem there will be deliverance, as the Lord has said, even among the survivors whom the Lord calls. (Joel 2:28-32)

God told Joel to write this during a time when Jerusalem and Judah were nearly devastated by an invasion of locusts and severe drought. Almost every level of society, both rich and poor, was deeply affected. It is well-documented that in both ancient times, and today, a large invasion of locusts can strip bare everything grown over many square miles.

Before God promises this spiritual outpouring, he promises that he will repay for all of the things that the locust devoured. Isn't it good to know that no matter what has been taken from us by sin or by life, God promises that he will not only renew us spiritually but physically as well?

This outpouring will only lead us to life more abundantly:

> The thief comes only to steal and kill and destroy; I have come that they may have life, and have it to the full. (John 10:10)

On the Day of Pentecost, this passage of Scripture from Joel is quoted to explain the outpouring of the Spirit on the disciples.

There are five key points in this passage:

1.) God promises to pour out his Spirit on "everyone who calls on the name of the Lord," both Jew and Gentile.

2.) It is an ongoing promise to everyone who will accept Christ as Lord. In other words, all believers can and should be filled with the Holy Spirit.

3.) This new impartation of the Spirit will release prophetic gifts, and the release of those gifts will make God's presence known among his people and also unbelievers.

But if an unbeliever or an inquirer comes in while everyone is prophesying, they are convicted of sin and are brought under judgment by all, as the secrets of their hearts are laid bare. So they will fall down and worship God, exclaiming, "God is really among you!" (1 Corinthians 14:24-25)

4.) Both men and woman will receive the Baptism of the Holy Spirit.

5.) When the full realization of the outpouring of the Spirit and the offer of salvation to all people has occurred, it will be followed by the end-time cosmic signs and the "day of the Lord."

Immediately after the distress of those days 'the sun will be darkened, and the moon will not give its light; the stars will fall from the sky, and the heavenly bodies

61

will be shaken.' Then will appear the sign of the Son of Man in heaven. And then all the peoples of the earth will mourn when they see the Son of Man coming on the clouds of heaven, with power and great glory. And he will send his angels with a loud trumpet call, and they will gather his elect from the four winds, from one end of the heavens to the other. (Matthew 24:29-31)

For a deeper study, here are more Old Testament Scriptures that talk about the Baptism of the Holy Spirit:

Exodus 31:1-6	Numbers 27:18
Judges 3:9-10	Judges 6:34
Judges 11:29	Judges 13:14-15
1 Samuel 11:6-7	1 Samuel 16:13
1 Chronicles 12:18	2 Chronicles 24:20-21
Psalm 51:10-12	Isaiah 11:1-3
Isaiah 42:1	Isaiah 59:21
Ezekiel 2:1-2	Ezekiel 11:19-20
Ezekiel 36:26-27	Ezekiel 37:14
Micah 3:8	Zechariah 4:6

DAY 5

JESUS AND THE BAPTISM OF THE HOLY SPIRIT: PART 1

I baptize you with water for repentance. But after me comes one who is more powerful than I, whose sandals I am not worthy to carry. He will baptize you with the Holy Spirit and fire. His winnowing fork is in his hand, and he will clear his threshing floor, gathering his wheat into the barn and burning up the chaff with unquenchable fire."

Then Jesus came from Galilee to the Jordan to be baptized by John. But John tried to deter him, saying, "I need to be baptized by you, and do you come to me?"

Jesus replied, "Let it be so now; it is proper for us to do this to fulfill all righteousness." Then John consented.

As soon as Jesus was baptized, he went up out of the water. At that moment heaven was opened, and he saw the Spirit of God descending like a dove and alighting on him. And a voice from heaven said, "This is my Son, whom I love; with him I am well pleased."
(Matthew 3:11-17)

In our passage today, we open up with John the Baptist preaching to the religious leaders of the day about what Jesus will do and teach. He tells them that Jesus will give them power to witness and live for him. Then, Jesus appears and requests to be baptized.

Some of you may be thinking the same thing I did as a young Christian when I first read this passage: "Wait a minute. If Jesus was sinless, why did he need to be baptized?"

The answer lies in the text:

1.) To fulfill all righteousness.

This means that he was publicly consecrated to God and his kingdom according to Leviticus 16:4, which was the requirement for priesthood:

He is to put on the sacred linen tunic, with linen undergarments next to his body; he is to tie the linen sash around him and put on the linen turban. These are sacred garments; so he must bathe himself with water before he puts them on." (Leviticus 16:4)

2.) To identify with sinners.

Although Jesus did not have any sin for which to repent, he became sin for us. Being baptized in water doesn't make you right with God; being baptized in water shows that you are right with God.

God made him who had no sin to be sin for us, so that in him we might become the righteousness of God. (2 Corinthians 5:21)

He himself bore our sins in his body on the tree, so that we might die to sins and live for righteousness; "by his wounds you have been healed." (1 Peter 2:24)

3.) To begin his preaching ministry and miracles.

Jesus did not preach or perform any miracles until after he was baptized. He would later challenge his disciples not to begin their teaching ministry until they did the same.

I am going to send you what my Father has promised; but stay in the city until you have been clothed with power from on high. (Luke 24:49)

By being baptized, Jesus modeled for us that everything he did—his preaching, healing, suffering, and victory—he did by the power of the Holy Spirit.

If Jesus could do nothing without the enablement of the Spirit, how much more do we need the enablement of the Holy Spirit in our lives?

DAY 6

JESUS AND THE BAPTISM OF THE HOLY SPIRIT: PART 2

Jesus, full of the Holy Spirit, returned from the Jordan and was led by the Spirit into the wilderness, where for forty days he was tempted by the devil. He ate nothing during those days, and at the end of them he was hungry. (Luke 4:1-2)

In today's text, we see that immediately after Jesus was baptized, he was led by the Holy Spirit into the desert, where he was tempted by the devil for forty days. Let's take a look at that encounter:

The devil said to him, "If you are the Son of God, tell this stone to become bread."

Jesus answered, "It is written: 'Man does not live on bread alone.'"

The devil led him up to a high place and showed him in an instant all the kingdoms of the world. And he said to him, "I will give you all their authority and splendor; it has been given to me, and I can give it to anyone I want to. If you worship me, it will all be yours."

Jesus answered, "It is written: 'Worship the Lord your God and serve him only.'"

The devil led him to Jerusalem and had him stand on the highest point of the temple. "If you are the Son of God," he said, "throw yourself down from here. For it is written: 'He will command his angels concerning you to guard you carefully; they will lift you up in their hands, so that you will not strike your foot against a stone.'"

Jesus answered, "It is said: 'Do not put the Lord your God to the test.'" When the devil had finished all this tempting, he left him until an opportune time.
(Luke 4:3-13)

It was only because Jesus was full of the Holy Spirit that he was able to face Satan squarely and resist the temptations that came his way. The temptations that Jesus faced are the same three that we face every day:

1.) The Lust of the Flesh

Jesus was hungry. He was a normal man who lived in a normal body with every physical need that we have as humans. But because he was filled with the Holy Spirit, he was able to withstand the temptation.

2.) The Lust of the Eyes

Satan had the authority to give Jesus all the kingdoms of the world because Adam had given over that authority to Satan when he sinned in the garden. But, Jesus was filled with the Spirit and let his desire for God supersede his desire for earthly things.

3.) The Pride of Life

Satan wanted Jesus to prove that he was the Son of God. Jesus knew he didn't have to prove anything to anyone because he was bold enough to believe what God said at his baptism just a few weeks earlier: "This is my Son, whom I love; with him I am well pleased."

Like Jesus, it is God's intention that we never face the forces of evil and sin without the power of the Spirit. We must be equipped with his fullness and follow his leading in order to be victorious against Satan.

DAY 7

JESUS AND THE BAPTISM OF THE HOLY SPIRIT: PART 3

If you love me, you will keep my commands. And I will ask the Father, and he will give you another Counselor to be with you forever.
(John 14:15-16 CSB)

Jesus said that he would ask the Father to give the Counselor to those who love him and take his Word seriously. Obviously, you fit into this category because you are reading this today.

He emphasizes the point "if you love me," which focuses on a continuing attitude of love and obedience. The blessings of God are conditional, but the love of God is unconditional.

Jesus calls the Holy Spirit "another Counselor." The Greek word for "another" is "allon" which means "another of the same kind." (The opposite of this in Greek is "heteros," which means "another of a different kind.") The use of "allon" in the text tells us that the Holy Spirit will continue what Jesus did while he was here on earth.

The word "counselor" in the Greek is "parakletos" which means "one called alongside to help." It is also used in describing someone as a strengthener, comforter, helper, advisor, advocate, intercessor, ally, and friend.

John also uses the word "parakletos" when he is describing Jesus:

My dear children, I write this to you so that you will not sin. But if anybody does sin, we have an advocate with the Father—Jesus Christ, the Righteous One. (1 John 2:1)

God's Word tells us that the Holy Spirit will be with us:

1.) To help and strengthen us.

But you will receive power when the Holy Spirit comes on you; and you will be my witnesses... (Acts 1:8)

2.) To teach us the true course of our lives.

But the Counselor, the Holy Spirit, whom the Father will send in my name, will teach you all things and remind you of everything I have told you. (John 14:26 CSB)

3.) To comfort us in difficult situations.

I will not leave you as orphans; I will come to you. (John 14:18)

4.) To intercede in prayer for us.

In the same way, the Spirit helps us in our weakness. We do not know what we ought to pray for, but the Spirit himself intercedes for us through wordless groans. And he who searches our hearts knows the mind of the Spirit, because the Spirit intercedes for God's people in accordance with the will of God. (Romans 8:26-27)

5.) To be a friend and to further our best interest.

...the Spirit of truth. The world cannot accept him, because it neither sees him nor knows him. But you know him, for he lives with you and will be in you. (John 14:17)

What a joy to know that the Holy Spirit is available to meet every need that we will experience in our lives.

DAY 8

JESUS AND THE BAPTISM OF THE HOLY SPIRIT: PART 4

...the Spirit of truth. The world cannot accept him, because it neither sees him nor knows him. But you know him, for he lives with you and will be in you. (John 14:17)

The Holy Spirit is called "the Spirit of truth" numerous times throughout Scripture. Other references speak to the opposite of the "spirit of error."

> When the Counselor comes, the one I will send to you from the Father—the Spirit of truth who proceeds from the Father—he will testify about me. (John 15:26 CSB)

> But when he, the Spirit of truth, comes, he will guide you into all the truth. He will not speak on his own; he will speak only what he hears, and he will tell you what is yet to come. (John 16:13)

> We are from God, and whoever knows God listens to us; but whoever is not from God does not listen to us. This is how we recognize the Spirit of truth and the spirit of falsehood. (1 John 4:6)

> This is the one who came by water and blood—Jesus Christ.He did not come by water only, but by water and blood. And it is the Spirit who testifies, because the Spirit is the truth. (1 John 5:6)

The reason the Holy Spirit is called the "Spirit of truth" is because he is the Spirit of Jesus, who is truth. Jesus said in John 14:6: "I am the way and the truth and the life."

Jesus takes us into truth. Because the Holy Spirit is the Spirit of truth, he enlightens the truth, exposes untruth, and guides believers into all truth.

DAY 9

JESUS AND THE BAPTISM OF THE HOLY SPIRIT: PART 5

...the Spirit of truth. The world cannot accept him, because it neither sees him nor knows him. But you know him, for he lives with you and will be in you. (John 14:17)

When Jesus describes the Holy Spirit as "the Spirit of truth," it is important to also understand the Holy Spirit will not operate where there is no truth. In other words, no truth equals no Holy Spirit.

We can never be willing to sacrifice truth for the sake of unity, love, or any other reason and expect God's Spirit to empower us. If we compromise truth, we deny the Spirit of truth that we claim lives inside of us. If we abandon truth, we abandon God. The Holy Spirit cannot be the Counselor of those who are in rebellion to God's Word or who are half-hearted in their commitment to the truth.

The Holy Spirit comes only to those who worship the Lord "in Spirit and in truth."

> God is spirit, and his worshipers must worship in the Spirit and in truth. (John 4:24)

When the Holy Spirit is leading—because he is truth—he makes us sensitive to our shortcomings. He doesn't do this because he is a divine party crasher. He only does this because he wants to reveal things to us and about us that will make us deeper, richer, and fuller human beings.

The best teachers are the ones who make us aware of all that is around us. When they point out things that we were not aware of, it changes our opinions about others, about situations, and about ourselves. When we analyze the details, hear the stories, and research the question behind the question and the statement behind the statement, it enlightens us and exposes the truth. In other words, it reveals the Holy Spirit.

Could this be one of the reasons why the New Testament church spent so much time hanging out together? It seems to me that the more we hear one another's stories, the more tolerant we are of one another.

Max Lucado once wrote, "God heals his family through his family."

Healing can only come from exposure. Exposure to the truth is exposure to the Holy Spirit.

DAY 10

JESUS AND THE BAPTISM OF THE HOLY SPIRIT: PART 6

...the Spirit of truth. The world cannot accept him, because it neither sees him nor knows him. But you know him, for he lives with you and will be in you. (John 14:17)

The text tells us the Holy Spirit will be with us and in us. Let that thought sink in for a moment.

Jesus was telling his disciples that the Holy Spirit lived with them, and that, in the future, he would be in them. This was fulfilled when he breathed on his disciples following his resurrection and said, "Receive the Holy Spirit" as recorded in John 20:22.

At that moment, the Holy Spirit entered in to live in the disciples. Only after they received the Holy Spirit were they able to enjoy the promises that were fulfilled by Jesus' death and resurrection. In other words, their spirits were "born again" or "resurrected."

When Jesus breathed on them, the disciples received the person of the Holy Spirit. The Holy Spirit began to make them new people.

When we are saved, we also receive the person of the Holy Spirit.

The Apostle Paul writes about this in his letter to the church at Corinth:

Therefore, if anyone is in Christ, he is a new creation.
The old has passed away; behold, the new has come.
(2 Corinthians 5:17)

On the Day of Pentecost, they received the power of the Holy Spirit:

All of them were filled with the Holy Spirit and began
to speak in other tongues as the Spirit enabled them.
(Acts 2:4)

When we are "filled" or "baptized" in the Holy Spirit, we receive the power to be his witnesses:

But you will receive power when the Holy Spirit comes
on you; and you will be my witnesses in Jerusalem,
and in all Judea and Samaria, and to the ends of the
earth. (Acts 1:8)

The Baptism of the Holy Spirit is a separate and distinct work in the life of every believer. These two distinct works are biblically normative and available today for all Christians.

As a youth pastor, I would phrase it this way to help students understand: When you receive salvation, the Holy Spirit becomes a resident—he lives in you. But when you are filled, the Holy Spirit becomes president—he not only lives in you, but he calls the shots.

Millions of Christians have found life much more enjoyable and fulfilling when the Holy Spirit is running things. You will, too!

DAY 11

HOW IS THE HOLY SPIRIT GIVEN? PART 1

Peter replied, "Repent and be baptized, every one of you, in the name of Jesus Christ for the forgiveness of your sins. And you will receive the gift of the Holy Spirit. The promise is for you and your children and for all who are far off—for all whom the Lord our God will call." With many other words he warned them; and he pleaded with them, "Save yourselves from this corrupt generation." (Acts 2:38-40)

But when they believed Philip as he proclaimed the good news of the kingdom of God and the name of Jesus Christ, they were baptized, both men and women. Simon himself believed and was baptized. And he followed Philip everywhere, astonished by the great signs and miracles he saw. When the apostles in Jerusalem heard that Samaria had accepted the word of God, they sent Peter and John to Samaria. When they arrived, they prayed for the new believers there that they might receive the Holy Spirit, because the Holy Spirit had not yet come on any of them; they had simply been baptized in the name of the Lord Jesus. Then Peter and John placed their hands on them, and they received the Holy Spirit. (Acts 8:12–17)

The first and most basic requirement for receiving the Baptism of the Holy Spirit is that we must "receive Jesus." When we receive Jesus as our Lord and Savior, then we are a candidate for the Baptism of the Holy Spirit.

In Acts 8:12-17, we see that the Samaritans had fully met the conditions for salvation before they received the Baptism of the Holy Spirit. They believed and were baptized. These two facts make it clear that they had genuinely received salvation.

A few days after the Samaritans were saved, Peter and John arrived and prayed for them to be filled with the Holy Spirit in the same way they had received the Baptism of the Holy Spirit on the Day of Pentecost. This again shows the "two-stage" experience of "believing" (salvation) and then "receiving" the Baptism of the Holy Spirit.

The two-stage experience was also shown in the life of Paul and later in the new believers at Ephesus in the book of Acts:

"Who are you, Lord?" Saul asked.

"I am Jesus, whom you are persecuting," he replied.

"Now get up and go into the city, and you will be told what you must do."

The men traveling with Saul stood there speechless; they heard the sound but did not see anyone. Saul got up from the ground, but when he opened his eyes he could see nothing. So they led him by the hand into Damascus.

For three days he was blind, and did not eat or drink anything.

In Damascus there was a disciple named Ananias. The Lord called to him in a vision, "Ananias!"

"Yes, Lord," he answered.

The Lord told him, "Go to the house of Judas on

Straight Street and ask for a man from Tarsus named Saul, for he is praying. In a vision he has seen a man named Ananias come and place his hands on him to restore his sight."

"Lord," Ananias answered, "I have heard many reports about this man and all the harm he has done to your holy people in Jerusalem. And he has come here with authority from the chief priests to arrest all who call on your name."

But the Lord said to Ananias, "Go! This man is my chosen instrument to proclaim my name to the Gentiles and their kings and to the people of Israel. I will show him how much he must suffer for my name."

Then Ananias went to the house and entered it. Placing his hands on Saul, he said, "Brother Saul, the Lord—Jesus, who appeared to you on the road as you were coming here—has sent me so that you may see again and be filled with the Holy Spirit." (Acts 9:5-17)

While Apollos was at Corinth, Paul took the road through the interior and arrived at Ephesus. There he found some disciples and asked them, "Did you receive the Holy Spirit when you believed?"

They answered, "No, we have not even heard that there is a Holy Spirit."

So Paul asked, "Then what baptism did you receive?"

"John's baptism," they replied.

Paul said, "John's baptism was a baptism of repentance. He told the people to believe in the one coming after him, that is, in Jesus." On hearing this, they were baptized in the name of the Lord Jesus. When Paul place his hands on them, the Holy Spirit came on them, and they spoke in tongues and prophesied. (Acts 19:1-6)

When we meet the first requirement, we then begin to see how easy it is to receive the fullness of the Holy Spirit.

DAY 12

HOW IS THE HOLY SPIRIT
GIVEN? PART 2

Peter replied, "Repent and be baptized, every one of you, in the name of Jesus Christ for the forgiveness of your sins. And you will receive the gift of the Holy Spirit. The promise is for you and your children and for all who are far off—for all whom the Lord our God will call." With many other words he warned them; and he pleaded with them, "Save yourselves from this corrupt generation."
(Acts 2:38-40)

After believing in Jesus and receiving him as our Savior and Lord, the next thing we must do in our pursuit of the Baptism of the Holy Spirit is to turn from sin and those things that grieve the heart of God.

Too many times, people say that they are a Christ follower, but they desire to continue living a life of sin. After salvation, we must begin our journey of following God and abandoning ourselves. Abandoning ourselves means that we begin to learn what displeases God, and upon learning these things, we act in accordance with what God wants, not what we want.

To receive the Baptism of the Holy Spirit, we don't have to be perfect; we just have to desire to be like Jesus and be willing to lay down our struggles and trust him to deliver us.

At a youth camp many years ago, I was praying for a young man to receive the Baptism of the Holy Spirit. We prayed for hours and hours, and I asked others to help me pray for this young man, yet he never received. I encouraged him to begin to study God's Word, and we would continue to pray.

When I followed up with him later on, he finally confessed that he was deeply involved in a strong arm of witchcraft. He wanted to be saved, but still wanted to be involved in this particular group that would role play in demonic activity. He was accepted in this group and did not know if it was sinful or not. I strongly urged him that if he wanted to receive the Baptism of the Holy Spirit, he would need to repent of this. I don't know if he ever did. I do know that it was God's desire to fill him, but he could not receive because of the sin in his life.

The key word in Holy Spirit is "holy." When we pursue his holiness, we will also receive his Spirit.

DAY 13

HOW IS THE HOLY SPIRIT GIVEN? PART 3

On the last and greatest day of the festival, Jesus stood and said in a loud voice, "Let anyone who is thirsty come to me and drink. Whoever believes in me, as Scripture has said, rivers of living water will flow from within them." By this he meant the Spirit, whom those who believed in him were later to receive. Up to that time the Spirit had not been given, since Jesus had not yet been glorified. (John 7:37-39)

Blessed are those who hunger and thirst for righteousness, for they will be filled. (Matthew 5:6)

But seek first his kingdom and his righteousness, and all these things will be given to you as well. (Matthew 6:33)

In order to receive the Baptism of the Holy Spirit, we need to desire to be filled. Obviously, over the last thirteen days, you have shown a desire by studying and reading these daily devotionals.

Too many people have taken the approach of "Well, if God wants to fill me, he will fill me."

What an unfortunate attitude to take regarding any area of your life, especially your spiritual life. Anything that we want to possess, we must pursue. As you pursue, you begin to see that God honors those who pursue him.

In Matthew 5:6 we learned that those who hunger and thirst

for righteousness will be filled. So, how do you know if you are hungry for something? Proverbs 16:26 says, "The appetite of laborers works for them; their hunger drives them on."

We begin to show our hunger in our pursuit of God by prayer and by asking God to fill us with his Holy Spirit. When there is an opportunity in your church to receive prayer to be filled with the Holy Spirit, respect it. When we are passionate for the things of God, God will respond.

> If you then, though you are evil, know how to give good gifts to your children, how much more will your Father in heaven give the Holy Spirit to those who ask him! (Luke 11:13)

> They all joined together constantly in prayer, along with the women and Mary the mother of Jesus, and with his brothers. (Acts 1:14)

> When the day of Pentecost came, they were all together in one place. Suddenly a sound like the blowing of a violent wind came from heaven and filled the whole house where they were sitting. They saw what seemed to be tongues of fire that separated and came to rest on each of them. All of them were filled with the Holy Spirit and began to speak in other tongues as the Spirit enabled them. (Acts 2:1-4)

> After they prayed, the place where they were meeting was shaken. And they were all filled with the Holy Spirit and spoke the word of God boldly. (Acts 4:31)

> When they arrived, they prayed for the new believers there that they might receive the Holy Spirit, because

the Holy Spirit had not yet come on any of them; they had simply been baptized in the name of the Lord Jesus. Then Peter and John placed their hands on them, and they received the Holy Spirit. (Acts 8:15-17)

DAY 14

HOW IS THE HOLY SPIRIT GIVEN? PART 4

Therefore I tell you, whatever you ask for in prayer, believe that you have received it, and it will be yours. (Mark 11:24)

On one occasion, while he was eating with them, he gave them this command: "Do not leave Jerusalem, but wait for the gift my Father promised, which you have heard me speak about. For John baptized with water, but in a few days you will be baptized with the Holy Spirit." (Acts 1:4-5)

In our pursuit of the Baptism of the Holy Spirit, the final requirement is that we expect to be filled. When you begin to expect God to fulfill his word in your life, a faith is imparted in your spirit that is from God himself.

Jesus spoke about what the Holy Spirit was going to do, but he didn't say when it would occur. The disciples obeyed what Jesus said to do, and then they were filled just a few days later. Sometimes God fulfills his word immediately. Other times, we must wait for the promise.

God rewards those who expect him to fulfill his word. In Matthew, Jesus told his disciples:

> Truly I tell you, if you have faith as small as a mustard seed, you can say to this mountain, 'Move from here to there,' and it will move. Nothing will be impossible for you. (Matthew 17:20)

The book of Hebrews shows us the heart of God toward his children regarding our expectancy of him:

> And without faith it is impossible to please God, because anyone who comes to him must believe that he exists and that he rewards those who earnestly seek him. (Hebrews 11:6)

In Acts, we see how the early church committed to the pursuit of God:

> They all joined together constantly in prayer, along with the women and Mary the mother of Jesus, and with his brothers (Acts 1:14)

Keep praying, keep studying, and keep expecting. This is a promised gift from God.

DAY 15

WHAT ABOUT SPEAKING IN TONGUES? PART 1

All of them were filled with the Holy Spirit and began to speak in other tongues as the Spirit enabled them. (Acts 2:4)

Speaking in other tongues was considered by New Testament Christians to be a God-given sign accompanying the Baptism of the Holy Spirit.

> The circumcised believers who had come with Peter were astonished that the gift of the Holy Spirit had been poured out even on Gentiles. For they heard them speaking in tongues and praising God. Then Peter said, "Surely no one can stand in the way of their being baptized with water. They have received the Holy Spirit just as we have." (Acts 10:45-47)

> When Paul placed his hands on them, the Holy Spirit came on them, and they spoke in tongues and prophesied." (Acts 19:6)

Speaking in tongues is a supernatural act of the Holy Spirit where a believer speaks in a language they have never learned. It may be an existing language here on earth or a heavenly one.

God has linked speaking in tongues with the Baptism of the Holy Spirit since the Day of Pentecost so that Christians could have a confirmation that they had received the Baptism of the Holy Spirit.

The purpose of the gift of tongues is to enable the believer to speak to God in our private prayer time to build up our spiritual life:

> Anyone who speaks in a tongue edifies themselves, but the one who prophesies edifies the church.
> (1 Corinthians 14:4)

Speaking in tongues is praying at the level of the Spirit:

> For anyone who speaks in a tongue does not speak to people but to God. Indeed, no one understands them; they utter mysteries by the Spirit. (1 Corinthians 14:2)

> For if I pray in a tongue, my spirit prays, but my mind is unfruitful. (1 Corinthians 14:14)

> So what shall I do? I will pray with my spirit, but I will also pray with my understanding... (1 Corinthians 14:15)

Speaking with other tongues can also be used for giving thanks:

> Otherwise when you are praising God in the Spirit, how can someone else, who is now put in the position of an inquirer, say "Amen" to your thanksgiving, since they do not know what you are saying? You are giving thanks well enough, but no one else is edified.
> (1 Corinthians 14:16-17)

It can also be used for singing:

> I will sing with my spirit, but I will also sing with my

understanding. (1 Corinthians 14:15)

Scripture gives us multiple uses for speaking in other tongues in our private prayer times to connect with God in intimate and personal ways.

DAY 16

WHAT ABOUT SPEAKING IN TONGUES? PART 2

I would like every one of you to speak in tongues, but I would rather have you prophesy. The one who prophesies is greater than the one who speaks in tongues, unless someone interprets, so that the church may be edified. Now, brothers and sisters, if I come to you and speak in tongues, what good will I be to you, unless I bring you some revelation or knowledge or prophecy or word of instruction?
(1 Corinthians 14:5-7)

For this reason the one who speaks in a tongue should pray that they may interpret what they say. For if I pray in a tongue, my spirit prays, but my mind is unfruitful. So what shall I do? I will pray with my spirit, but I will also pray with my understanding; I will sing with my spirit, but I will also sing with my understanding. Otherwise when you are praising God in the Spirit, how can someone else, who is now put in the position of an inquirer, say "Amen" to your thanksgiving, since they do not know what you are saying? You are giving thanks well enough, but no one else is edified
(1 Corinthians 14:13-17)

Yesterday, we discussed speaking in other tongues as a part of a believer's personal prayer time with God. However, many have confused the Baptism of the Holy Spirit with a public message given in tongues accompanied by an interpretation of the unknown language.

This particular event that Paul is talking about is one of the nine supernatural gifts of the Holy Spirit. When this gift of tongues is given, an interpretation must also follow so that the audience can understand the meaning and context and apply it to their lives. It is a completely separate event from the Baptism of the Holy Spirit.

The Baptism of the Holy Spirit was not just given so that we could participate in public service, but also for public and private prayer. The experience helps you in so many ways that it can't be limited just to a message in tongues.

The Bible says that there are so many different functions to what happens when we speak in other tongues that as we are doing it, we are "speaking mysteries to our spirit." There are mysteries that God wants to unlock in his Word so that our lives will be rich and full.

One time when I was studying God's Word, I asked God, "Why tongues? Why not something else?" The Holy Spirit showed me that the reason why God wants to use our tongues is because this is the area where we struggle the most.

> Likewise, the tongue is a small part of the body, but it makes great boasts. Consider what a great forest is set on fire by a small spark. The tongue also is a fire, a world of evil among the parts of the body. It corrupts the whole body, sets the course of one's life on fire, and is itself set on fire by hell. All kinds of animals, birds, reptiles and sea creatures are being tamed and have been tamed by mankind, but no human being can tame the tongue. It is a restless evil, full of deadly poison. With the tongue we praise our Lord and Father, and with it we curse human beings, who have been made in God's likeness. Out of the same mouth come praise and cursing. My brothers and sisters, this should not be. Can both fresh water and salt water flow from the same spring? My brothers and sisters,

can a fig tree bear olives, or a grapevine bear figs? Neither can a salt spring produce fresh water. (James 3:5-12)

The weapon that can cause the most damage to ourselves and to others is also the weapon that we can use to tear down the plans of the enemy. Isn't it just like God to turn the tables on the devil with his own tricks?

DAY 17

THE SPIRIT-FILLED LIFESTYLE: PART 1

On their release, Peter and John went back to their own people and reported all that the chief priests and elders had said to them. When they heard this, they raised their voices together in prayer to God. "Sovereign Lord," they said, "you made the heaven and the earth and the sea, and everything in them. You spoke by the Holy Spirit through the mouth of your servant, our father David: 'Why do the nations rage and the peoples plot in vain? The kings of the earth rise up and the rulers band together against the Lord and against his anointed one.' Indeed Herod and Pontius Pilate met together with the Gentiles and the people of Israel in this city to conspire against your holy servant Jesus, whom you anointed. They did what your power and will had decided beforehand should happen. Now, Lord, consider their threats and enable your servants to speak your word with great boldness. Stretch out your hand to heal and perform signs and wonders through the name of your holy servant Jesus." After they prayed, the place where they were meeting was shaken. And they were all filled with the Holy Spirit and spoke the word of God boldly. (Acts 4:23-31)

What will speaking in other tongues produce in our life? One of the first things it will produce is a stronger desire to pray.

Before I received the Baptism of the Holy Spirit, I only prayed when I wanted something or was in trouble and needed God's help. The day after I was filled with the Holy Spirit, I went to work outside in the south Alabama heat, and I prayed all day in tongues and in English. I had a special sense that God was with me and I just wanted to talk to him. Before that day, I would have needed a radio or someone else to talk to, or I would've just goofed off. But that particular day just flew by as I spent one-on-one time with God in prayer.

In our passage today, we see that Peter and John were on their way to the temple when God used them to bring the gift of healing to a man. The religious people of the day began to persecute them because Peter and John spoke about Jesus when the man was healed. They were arrested and put in jail for a miracle.

Now, just before this, Peter and John were so afraid of these religious leaders that they locked themselves in a room in hiding. After being filled with the Holy Spirit, they had the courage to defy their persecutors and continue to boldly preach in Jesus' name.

Notice how much they had matured since their days with Jesus. They weren't bragging about how great they were. They went back and called a prayer meeting so that they would continue to be bold and so that the signs, wonders, and healings could increase and continue. The Baptism of the Holy Spirit gave them boldness but also gave them a greater desire for God's presence in and on their lives.

Here are some other examples of an increased desire to pray as a result of the filling of the Spirit:

> Those who accepted his message were baptized, and about three thousand were added to their number that day. They devoted themselves to the apostles' teaching and to fellowship, to the breaking of bread and to prayer. (Acts 2:41-42)

One day Peter and John were going up to the temple at the time of prayer—at three in the afternoon. (Acts 3:1)

We will turn this responsibility over to them and will give our attention to prayer and the ministry of the word. (Acts 6:3-4)

About noon the following day as they were on their journey and approaching the city, Peter went up on the roof to pray. (Acts 10:9)

In the same way, the Spirit helps us in our weakness. We do not know what we ought to pray for, but the Spirit himself intercedes for us through wordless groans. (Romans 8:26)

DAY 18

THE SPIRIT-FILLED LIFESTYLE: PART 2

When he comes, he will prove the world to be in the wrong about sin and righteousness and judgment. (John 16:8)

But you will receive power when the Holy Spirit comes on you; and you will be my witnesses in Jerusalem, and in all Judea and Samaria, and to the ends of the earth. (Acts 1:8)

Along with a greater desire to pray, the Baptism of the Holy Spirit also will produce an enhanced sensitivity to sin.

When we sin, we will not only know it, but we will be bothered by it like never before. We will love the communication with God and his presence so much that we will not want to do anything to hinder that intimacy. We will begin to experience conviction in areas where we were once calloused. We will begin to choose our spiritual desires over our natural ones. We will develop an intolerance for continual disobedience in our lives.

As we live the Spirit-filled life, we will begin to realize that we must choose to surrender more of ourselves to receive more of God. If we remain stubborn and decide to try and play both sides, we will quickly find ourselves at a crossroads. We will choose one or the other. Much like the addict who needs more of the drug to produce the needed effect, we will know that we will have to sacrifice more to continue to grow.

Once you have discovered this closeness with God, you can never go back to the way things used to be.

DAY 19

THE SPIRIT-FILLED LIFESTYLE: PART 3

But when he, the Spirit of truth, comes, he will guide you into all the truth. He will not speak on his own; he will speak only what he hears, and he will tell you what is yet to come. (John 16:13)

They devoted themselves to the apostles' teaching and to fellowship, to the breaking of bread and to prayer. (Acts 2:42)

A Spirit-filled life will also produce a deeper love for God's Word.

As a pastor, I love to preach and teach God's Word. The hunger for God's Word in the lives of those who are filled with his Spirit is fascinating to witness. People who at one time would sit through a church service with little to no expression on their face, now begin to sit on the edge of their seat and hang on every word of Scripture.

I realize that there are some people who are born students and just love to listen to teaching of any kind. They naturally have a great desire to learn. Those are not the ones I'm referring to.

The Apostle Paul spoke in Athens about Christ to men who didn't believe in Jesus but enjoyed hearing new ideas:

All the Athenians and the foreigners who lived there spent their time doing nothing but talking about and listening to the latest ideas. (Acts 17:21)

When you become filled with the Holy Spirit, your desire for the Word of God will increase because you want to learn more about him and how you can continue to grow in your spiritual journey.

The Bible talks about how you can have more power and more understanding of the Word of God because the Holy Spirit speaks to you through the Word of God.

The Word and the Spirit don't compete with each other—they complement each other.

When we think the Holy Spirit has spoken to us about something, we then check it out and see if it lines up with God's Word. If it doesn't, it wasn't the Holy Spirit. The Word and the Spirit mirror each other.

DAY 20

THE SPIRIT-FILLED LIFESTYLE: PART 4

All of them were filled with the Holy Spirit and began to speak in other tongues as the Spirit enabled them. (Acts 2:4)

In the last days, God says, I will pour out my Spirit on all people. Your sons and daughters will prophesy, your young men will see visions, your old men will dream dreams. (Acts 2:17)

For they heard them speaking in tongues and praising God. (Acts 10:46)

For anyone who speaks in a tongue does not speak to people but to God. Indeed, no one understands them; they utter mysteries by the Spirit. (1 Corinthians 14:2)

Another part of the Spirit-filled life is what Scripture refers to as prophetic utterances and declarations of praise.

There have been so many times since the day I received the Baptism of the Holy Spirit that I have said, "Wow, where did that come from?"

When you begin to recall things that you have read in your quiet times with God or speak the truths of your heart that seem to have come out of nowhere, you have just been used in a prophetic utterance.

Utterance means "words from within." When we read God's Word, we file away the truths of Scripture, which come alive when we need them.

Often when I preach, I will begin to bring up a point that is not outlined in my notes, but I can see by the reaction of the congregation that it needed to be said even though I had not planned to say it. I then recall John 14:26:

> But the Counselor, the Holy Spirit, whom the Father will send in my name, will teach you all things and remind you of everything I have told you. (John 14:26 CSB)

The declarations of praise aren't usually an intentional expression but rather flow naturally out of your spirit.

Sometimes when I am driving or going about my day, I just say, "I love you, Lord. Thank you. You are so awesome." Not as a result of anything in particular, but just because I'm overwhelmed by his presence. Or, at times, I catch myself praying in tongues and not even realizing it. It happened just earlier today as I was worshipping.

God wants us to worship and pray all day and our prayer language helps us to do just that.

DAY 21

THE SPIRIT-FILLED LIFESTYLE: PART 5

There are different kinds of gifts, but the same Spirit distributes them. There are different kinds of service, but the same Lord. There are different kinds of working, but in all of them and in everyone it is the same God at work. Now to each one the manifestation of the Spirit is given for the common good. To one there is given through the Spirit a message of wisdom, to another a message of knowledge by means of the same Spirit, to another faith by the same Spirit, to another gifts of healing by that one Spirit, to another miraculous powers, to another prophecy, to another distinguishing between spirits, to another speaking in different kinds of tongues, and to still another the interpretation of tongues. (1 Corinthians 12:4-10)

When we are filled with the Holy Spirit, we begin to desire supernatural things.

The following are the nine supernatural gifts that the Holy Spirit uses and operates in a public or church setting:

1.) The Word of Wisdom

This is different from wisdom learned through study and prayer. This is a message about an event usually in the past of a particular individual that you were never told about. It applies the wisdom of God's Word to the problem.

2.) The Word of Knowledge

This is a word that reveals specific knowledge about

people, circumstances, or biblical truth that you did not originally know.

3.) The Gift of Faith

This is a supernatural faith that enables the believer to believe God in desperate situations.

4.) Gifts of Healings

All Christians should pray for the sick to be healed. However, this gift of healing supernaturally takes place instantly.

5.) Gifts of Miracles

This is a supernatural power that alters the course of nature.

6.) Word of Prophecy

This is the gift that enables the believer to bring a word of revelation directly under the guidance of the Holy Spirit.

7.) The Discerning of Spirits

This is the ability to judge spirits or prophesies and to distinguish whether it is from the Holy Spirit or not.

8.) A Message in Tongues

This is a message that is given in a language that neither the speaker nor the audience know. An interpretation must follow this public message in tongues.

9.) Interpretation of Tongues

This is the ability to understand and communicate the meaning of a message in tongues.

When God baptizes us in his Holy Spirit, our spirit is awakened to the supernatural, and we must begin to study how God wants to use us in these gifts in the days to come.

DAY 22

THE SPIRIT-FILLED LIFESTYLE: PART 6

On one occasion, while he was eating with them, he gave them this command: "Do not leave Jerusalem, but wait for the gift my Father promised, which you have heard me speak about."
(Acts 1:4)

The Spirit you received does not make you slaves, so that you live in fear again; rather, the Spirit you received brought about your adoption to sonship. And by him we cry, "Abba, Father."
(Romans 8:15)

Because you are his sons, God sent the Spirit of his Son into our hearts, the Spirit who calls out, "Abba, Father." (Galatians 4:6)

For some, this particular work that the Baptism of the Holy Spirit brings is perhaps the most significant. As we live the Spirit-filled life, we begin to know God as our Father.

Personally, I think I was born with the world's greatest dad. However, when I was filled with the Holy Spirit, I immediately began to depend upon God much like a newborn baby. From deliverance from the strongholds of addiction, to deciding what college to attend, I desperately depended on God for everything.

Only years after I began to grow spiritually did I realize that this was a characteristic of the Spirit-filled life.

When God's Word says that we have received the "Spirit of sonship," it means he truly desires to bond with us, put his

Spirit in us, and deliver us from the spirit of fear that comes from the enemy.

The words "Abba Father" mean that you begin to know God as a dad in your life. You bond with him. You know his likes and dislikes. You enjoy hanging out with him and you begin to act like him.

I once knew a couple from India who had the cutest little girl. She did not call her father "dad" like most Americans. Instead, she called him "Appa," which meant the same thing in India. Whenever I read these verses, I think of her, and I try to relate to God like she did to her father.

DAY 23

THE RIVER OF REVIVAL: PART 1

*On the last and greatest day of the festival, Jesus stood and said
in a loud voice, "Let anyone who is thirsty come to me and drink.
Whoever believes in me, as Scripture has said, rivers of living water
will flow from within them." By this he meant the Spirit, whom
those who believed in him were later to receive. Up to that time the
Spirit had not been given, since Jesus had not yet been glorified.
(John 7:37-39)*

As Jesus spoke these words to the crowded streets of Jerusalem, it was on the eighth day of the Feast of Tabernacles.

If you're not familiar with Jewish culture, the Feast of Tabernacles is the only feast where outsiders are invited to join in. All over the city, tents and booths are set up for everyone to join in the festivities.

One of the best things about this particular festival is that is lasts eight days. A friend of mine who was in Jerusalem during this feast described it like this: "It is Thanksgiving, Christmas, 4th of July, your birthday, and your family reunion all wrapped up into one holiday, non-stop for eight straight days."

I thought to myself, "Man, my Jewish brothers really know how to party!"

With all of the dancing and celebrating, along with eating and drinking, it doesn't make any logical sense for Jesus to shout at the top of his lungs, "Let anyone who is thirsty come to me and drink." The place was filled with an abundance of food and drink. If you were thirsty, you could just go to a tent and get whatever type of drink you wanted.

Our text shows us that what Jesus meant by thirst was spiritual thirst that can't be quenched by anything but the Spirit of God. In seeing all of the people going back and forth from the temple area and knowing their desire for more of God, could it be that Jesus was able to sympathize with their spiritual frustration to such a point that he was filled with compassion and the desire to meet the dryness of their spirits with the refreshing work of the Holy Spirit? Scripture confirms that spiritual thirst was exactly what Jesus was referring to.

When we are dry and overwhelmed, the Spirit of God will renew and refresh us with more than enough of what we could ever need. Rivers supply more than enough water for us and others. The Baptism of the Holy Spirit allows us to draw from the spiritual river of renewal and be strengthened by it.

DAY 24

THE RIVER OF REVIVAL: PART 2

*On the last and greatest day of the festival, Jesus stood and said
in a loud voice, "Let anyone who is thirsty come to me and drink.
Whoever believes in me, as Scripture has said, rivers of living water
will flow from within them." By this he meant the Spirit, whom
those who believed in him were later to receive. Up to that time the
Spirit had not been given, since Jesus had not yet been glorified.*
(John 7:37-39)

During the Feast of Tabernacles, there are several key events
that occur. Jesus references them in his declaration in
today's text.

Near the temple in Jerusalem was the Pool of Siloam. The
water that came out of it was referred to by the Jews as
"living water" because of its proximity to the temple. Their
reference to it as "living water" meant the water was given
by God rather than drawn and carried by humans to the
place it was needed.

The Pool of Siloam was a man-made pool of water that was
built in 700 B.C. Jerusalem was not built near a large body
of water, and when the city was surrounded by its enemies,
some Israelite men tunneled through the middle of the city
to an outside body of water that actually brought water
right in the middle of the city.

The word "Siloam" actually means "sent forth," which is
figurative language for the life-changing power of the Holy
Spirit.

When Jesus spoke of the "living water," he was saying that the Holy Spirit was going to provide a way for all of us to renew ourselves on the inside as Christians. He goes on to emphasize that what the Holy Spirit would provide would not be a pool but a river. Pools can be privately owned, but rivers are for everyone.

God knows that we as Christians can become weary. And, if we can't refresh and renew ourselves from time to time, we won't be able to fulfill the mission that he has purposed for our life.

> For anyone who speaks in a tongue does not speak to people but to God. Indeed, no one understands them; they utter mysteries by the Spirit. But the one who prophesies speaks to people for their strengthening, encouragement and comfort. Anyone who speaks in a tongue edifies themselves, but the one who prophesies edifies the church. (1 Corinthians 14:2-4)

The passage above says to us that this "strengthening" can take place when we speak with other tongues. Speaking with other tongues as a part of our private devotional time with God renews us and builds us up.

The Pool of Siloam was a picture of the rivers that flow from within because it ran deep through the heart of the city, just like the Holy Spirit is not seen from the outside but on the inside of our hearts.

DAY 25

THE RIVER OF REVIVAL: PART 3

*On the last and greatest day of the festival, Jesus stood and said
in a loud voice, "Let anyone who is thirsty come to me and drink.
Whoever believes in me, as Scripture has said, rivers of living water
will flow from within them." By this he meant the Spirit, whom
those who believed in him were later to receive. Up to that time the
Spirit had not been given, since Jesus had not yet been glorified.*
(John 7:37-39)

During the Feast of Tabernacles, on the last day, which is
the eighth day, a very significant evening event takes place
that helps us understand this passage of Scripture in greater
depth.

In the Greek alphabet, every letter has a number, and every
letter that makes up a name has a numerical value. In the
Bible, the number eight is always associated with new beginnings.

On the eighth day of the festival, the Jewish people would
have a ceremony called "The Pouring of the Water." The
temple workers would go down to the Pool of Siloam and
take a golden vessel from the temple and fill the vessel with
water. After filling the vessel with water, they would go to
the altar, climb to the highest point of the temple, and pour
the water ("living water" as it was known) on the temple
steps.

When the water would hit the temple steps, the people
would begin to celebrate and praise God with all of their
hearts. As a drink offering on the altar, it signaled the begin-

ning of prayers for the rains for the next season's crops that would be needed to sustain the lives of God's people. It was also important because it was a reminder of God's promise to one day pour out his Spirit upon all people. The people would celebrate what would later come to pass on the Day of Pentecost.

That day, Jesus was letting the people know that all of his followers would be able to receive the Spirit of God to refresh, renew, and restore them. The Spirit of God is always associated with new beginnings, and God has a new beginning for all of us.

DAY 26

THE RIVER OF REVIVAL: PART 4

As he went along, he saw a man blind from birth. His disciples asked him, "Rabbi, who sinned, this man or his parents, that he was born blind?"

"Neither this man nor his parents sinned," said Jesus, "but this happened so that the works of God might be displayed in his life. As long as it is day, we must do the works of him who sent me. Night is coming, when no one can work. While I am in the world, I am the light of the world."

After saying this, he spit on the ground, made some mud with the saliva, and put it on the man's eyes. "Go," he told him, "wash in the Pool of Siloam." So the man went and washed, and came home seeing. (John 9:1-7)

As we finish our study on "the Spirit of renewal," we again see the Jewish reference to the Pool of Siloam, but this time in a different setting.

Why do you think Jesus told the man to go and wash in the Pool of Siloam?

As Jesus made mud with the spit on the ground, he was setting a pattern for us to notice.

In the Bible, mud or clay is a symbol of humanity. Too many times we can get distracted because we get "man" in our eyes. When we begin to see the faults in others, or when others hurt us or talk bad about us, we can begin to get "clay" in our eyes.

The Holy Spirit is here to help work out all the distractions and frustrations. He has given us the ability to refresh ourselves.

There are a few common frustrations in everyone's lives:

1.) We can become weary of our natural surroundings. This is why it is so important to take vacations and get away for a while so that you can really begin to enjoy where you live when you get home.

2.) We can become weary of our activities. This is why God created a day of rest so that our bodies and minds can be renewed.

3.) Finally, we can become weary of human relationships. God doesn't want us to live a life of isolation, but relationships can be challenging.

Romans 5:5 tells us that God's love has been poured into our hearts through the Holy Spirit. God loves us so much that he wants us to be able to refresh ourselves so that we can love people like he loves them.

Jude 1:20 tells us that we can build ourselves up when we pray in the Spirit. When we pray in the Spirit and ask God to renew us, he can build up anything that we need back in our life.

Whatever challenge you might be facing, you can be renewed and built up when you set aside time to pray in other tongues and renew yourself spiritually.

DAY 27

THE FOUR RIVERS OF THE HOLY SPIRIT

A river watering the garden flowed from Eden; from there it was separated into four headwaters. The name of the first is the Pishon; it winds through the entire land of Havilah, where there is gold. (The gold of that land is good; aromatic resin and onyx are also there.) The name of the second river is the Gihon; it winds through the entire land of Cush. The name of the third river is the Tigris; it runs along the east side of Ashur. And the fourth river is the Euphrates. (Genesis 2:10-14)

In today's text, we read about the Garden of Eden, which many people may be surprised to learn represents a picture of the church today.

The river that flows through the garden also waters the garden (or church). That river is a picture of the Holy Spirit. The river separates into four headwaters, which correlate with the four functions of the Holy Spirit.

Today, the Old Testament serves as a picture to help us understand more about the New Testament and its application to our lives. For example, all of the physical battles in the Old Testament symbolize the battles we will fight spiritually in the New Testament.

As St. Augustine said in describing the blending of the Old Testament with the New Testament: "In the Old Testament the New is concealed, in the New the Old is revealed."

The four headwaters of the Holy Spirit also describe for us what happens to us when we speak in other tongues.

1.) The Pishon River

In Hebrew, it means "to grow up and be made fat." This is describing the Holy Spirit's ability to encourage, renew, and build us up.

2.) The Gihon River

In Hebrew, it means "to labor to bring forth." This is describing the Holy Spirit's power to reveal things to us in our spirit and in God's Word.

3.) The Hiddekel/Tigris River

In Hebrew, it means "to rush forth violently." This is describing the explosive and dynamic power of the Holy Spirit.

4.) The Euphrates River

In Hebrew, it means "to hold back." This is describing the Holy Spirit's help for us in intercession or prayer for others.

All through Scripture, God weaves the pictures and analogies about the Holy Spirit to illustrate how this applies to our lives. Our God is the God of pictures, stories, words, signs, and wonders so that we can know and better understand his Word and his ways.

DAY 28

CLOTHED WITH POWER

But you will receive power when the Holy Spirit comes on you; and you will be my witnesses in Jerusalem, and in all Judea and Samaria, and to the ends of the earth. (Acts 1:8)

This verse is the verse that the entire book of Acts revolves around. The main purpose for the Baptism of the Holy Spirit is to receive power to witness for Christ. The end result of our witness is so that Christ would be known, loved, and praised.

The word "power" in the Greek is the word "dunamis." When Alfred Nobel wanted a name for his new invention, he used a version of this word and called his invention "dynamite." This word described the explosive power of his invention and also describes the power of God. "Dunamis" means more than just strength or ability—it also means "power in action and in operation."

This power operated in Jesus so that he could drive out evil spirits and heal the sick.

> Jesus returned to Galilee in the power of the Spirit, and news about him spread through the whole countryside. (Luke 4:14)

> The Spirit of the Lord is on me, because he has anointed me to proclaim good news to the poor. He has sent me to proclaim freedom for the prisoners and recovery of sight for the blind, to set the oppressed free...(Luke 4:18)

All the people were amazed and said to each other, "What words these are! With authority and power he gives orders to impure spirits and they come out!" (Luke 4:36)

...who had come to hear him and to be healed of their diseases. Those troubled by impure spirits were cured, and the people all tried to touch him, because power was coming from him and healing them all." (Luke 6:18-19)

When Jesus had called the Twelve together, he gave them power and authority to drive out all demons and to cure diseases, and he sent them out to proclaim the kingdom of God and to heal the sick. (Luke 9:1-2)

This power also operated in the disciples so that they could do the same thing.

Now Stephen, a man full of God's grace and power, performed great wonders and signs among the people. (Acts 6:8)

Those who had been scattered preached the word wherever they went. Philip went down to a city in Samaria and proclaimed the Messiah there. When the crowds heard Philip and saw the signs he performed, they all paid close attention to what he said. For with shrieks, impure spirits came out of many, and many who were paralyzed or lame were healed. So there was great joy in that city. (Acts 8:4-8)

But when they believed Philip as he proclaimed the good news of the kingdom of God and the name of Jesus Christ, they were baptized, both men and women.

Simon himself believed and was baptized. And he followed Philip everywhere, astonished by the great signs and miracles he saw. (Acts 8:12-13)

...how God anointed Jesus of Nazareth with the Holy Spirit and power, and how he went around doing good and healing all who were under the power of the devil, because God was with him. (Acts 10:38)

So Paul and Barnabas spent considerable time there, speaking boldly for the Lord, who confirmed the message of his grace by enabling them to perform signs and wonders. (Acts 14:3)

Paul entered the synagogue and spoke boldly there for three months, arguing persuasively about the kingdom of God. But some of them became obstinate; they refused to believe and publicly maligned the Way. So Paul left them. He took the disciples with him and had discussions daily in the lecture hall of Tyrannus. This went on for two years, so that all the Jews and Greeks who lived in the province of Asia heard the word of the Lord. God did extraordinary miracles through Paul, so that even handkerchiefs and aprons that had touched him were taken to the sick, and their illnesses were cured and the evil spirits left them. (Acts 19:8-12)

The Baptism of the Holy Spirit is God's provision for releasing the power of the Holy Spirit in the life of every follower of Christ.

DAY 29

POWER TO WITNESS

But you will receive power when the Holy Spirit comes on you; and you will be my witnesses in Jerusalem, and in all Judea and Samaria, and to the ends of the earth. (Acts 1:8)

There are many people who share their faith in Christ but do not speak with other tongues. One of the greatest soul winners in the world was Billy Graham. Billy Graham had the spiritual calling to be an evangelist, and he never experienced speaking in tongues. His calling by God was supernatural, and he was effective because of his calling and God-given gifts at birth.

But what about those who are not called to full-time evangelism? Why do we need the extra power?

The Baptism of the Holy Spirit not only gives us the power to preach and be a witness for Christ, but it also increases our effectiveness as we do it. We are strengthened because our relationship with God is deepening as we grow in our time with him.

> But the Counselor, the Holy Spirit, whom the Father will send in my name, will teach you all things and remind you of everything I have told you. (John 14:26 CSB)

> When the Counselor comes, the one I will send to you from the Father—the Spirit of truth who proceeds from the Father—he will testify about me. You also will testify, because you have been with me from the

beginning. (John 15:26-27)

When we receive the Baptism of the Holy Spirit, it will be evident through our words and deeds. God's Spirit will begin to show us how to love and how to live out the example Jesus set for us.

DAY 30

FRESH FILLINGS

Then Peter, filled with the Holy Spirit, said to them... (Acts 4:8)

Being filled with the Holy Spirit is more than just a one-time experience. It's an ongoing work.

On this particular day, Peter received a fresh filling from the Holy Spirit that brought sudden inspiration, wisdom, and boldness enabling him to proclaim the truth of God.

Fresh fillings of the Holy Spirit are part of God's plan for everyone who has received the Baptism of the Holy Spirit.

Peter had been previously filled with the Holy Spirit and was freshly filled this day in order to rise to the new challenge before him.

We find this pattern all throughout the book of Acts:

> After they prayed, the place where they were meeting was shaken. And they were all filled with the Holy Spirit and spoke the word of God boldly. (Acts 4:31)

> But Stephen, full of the Holy Spirit, looked up to heaven and saw the glory of God, and Jesus standing at the right hand of God. (Acts 7:55)

> Then Saul, who was also called Paul, filled with the Holy Spirit, looked straight at Elymas and said... (Acts 13:9)

And the disciples were filled with joy and with the Holy Spirit. (Acts 13:52)

For this reason I kneel before the Father, from whom every family in heaven and on earth derives its name. I pray that out of his glorious riches he may strengthen you with power through his Spirit in your inner being, so that Christ may dwell in your hearts through faith. And I pray that you, being rooted and established in love, may have power, together with all the Lord's holy people, to grasp how wide and long and high and deep is the love of Christ, and to know this love that surpasses knowledge—that you may be filled to the measure of all the fullness of God. (Ephesians 3:14-19)

We should be continuously filled with the Spirit because we are continuously:

1.) Drilled

Satan never stops attacking, so we must continuously be renewed in order to match his fight.

2.) Spilled

As Christians, we are called to find an area of ministry where we can serve God to the best of our abilities. However, this type of service ministry is not a source for renewal. We are renewed when we are ministered to during our private devotion times with God and during corporate worship times.

3.) Stilled

The enemy wants to keep you stagnant and immobile. When we ask God for a fresh filling of his Spirit, we will then have the faith to follow Christ wherever he leads us.

Thank God for the daily work of the Holy Spirit!

DAY 31

CORPORATE FILLINGS

After they prayed, the place where they were meeting was shaken.
And they were all filled with the Holy Spirit and spoke the word of
God boldly. (Acts 4:31)

Yesterday, we discussed how the Baptism of the Holy Spirit is a repetitive work in the life of Christians. Fresh fillings are part of God's plan for our lives. However, in today's text, we see that God not only wants to give individual believers a fresh filling of his Spirit, but he also wants to fill his entire church.

In order for us to fulfill our mission, God not only needs to fill individuals, but he wants entire congregations to experience repeated visitations of his Spirit when special needs and challenges are presented.

Other accounts in the book of Acts show a pattern that follows the one we read about today:

> All of them were filled with the Holy Spirit and began to speak in other tongues as the Spirit enabled them. (Acts 2:4)

> And the disciples were filled with joy and with the Holy Spirit. (Acts 13:52)

When God moves on an entire congregation with a renewed filling of the Holy Spirit, it will produce a greater boldness and power to witness. It also produces a greater love for one other because, when we all have the mind of God, we are committed to unity.

Corporate fillings produce a greater understanding of what Christ did for us so that we can believe that God can do the same for others.

DAY 32

INTENSITY

On their release, Peter and John went back to their own people and reported all that the chief priests and elders had said to them. When they heard this, they raised their voices together in prayer to God. "Sovereign Lord," they said, "you made the heaven and the earth and the sea, and everything in them. You spoke by the Holy Spirit through the mouth of your servant, our father David: 'Why do the nations rage and the peoples plot in vain? The kings of the earth rise up and the rulers band together against the Lord and against his anointed one.' Indeed Herod and Pontius Pilate met together with the Gentiles and the people of Israel in this city to conspire against your holy servant Jesus, whom you anointed. They did what your power and will had decided beforehand should happen. Now, Lord, consider their threats and enable your servants to speak your word with great boldness. Stretch out your hand to heal and perform signs and wonders through the name of your holy servant Jesus." After they prayed, the place where they were meeting was shaken. And they were all filled with the Holy Spirit and spoke the word of God boldly. (Acts 4:23-31)

Today, let's discuss the three characteristics that every Spirit-filled Christian will possess.

1.) An ability to focus.

Peter and John were used by the Holy Spirit to bring about a work of healing in a man's body. They heard the voice of God because of their focus that day. They were on their way to a time of prayer and ministered to a hurting man. Spirit-filled Christians know how to focus on Jesus' ways, his words, and his weapons. We see that

Jesus spent time in prayer so that he would know God's plan for him.

Paul later writes about how to use this focus to battle the lies of the devil:

For though we live in the world, we do not wage war as the world does. The weapons we fight with are not the weapons of the world. On the contrary, they have divine power to demolish strongholds. We demolish arguments and every pretension that sets itself up against the knowledge of God, and we take captive every thought to make it obedient to Christ. (2 Corinthians 10:3-5)

2.) A willingness to fight.

The disciples knew they needed supernatural strength from God to fight this battle. They learned their lesson from the night in Gethsemane. This time, they didn't sleep, but immediately went to prayer. Their minds were focused, and so their answers were clear.

But Peter and John replied, "Which is right in God's eyes: to listen to you, or to him? You be the judges! As for us, we cannot help speaking about what we have seen and heard." (Acts 4:19-20)

When they were threatened, they asked for a fresh filling from God so they could continue to be bold. They no longer trusted themselves; they trusted the Holy Spirit and relied upon him.

3.) A commitment to pursue the fresh filling of God's Spirit.

The early church showed us that for every fight, there is a fresh filling from the Holy Spirit to win that fight and to see the power of the Holy Spirit prevail time and time again in our lives.

DAY 33

FULL OF THE SPIRIT

Brothers and sisters, choose seven men from among you who are known to be full of the Spirit and wisdom. We will turn this responsibility over to them. (Acts 6:3)

In choosing men to help carry out the work of a growing church, the early Christians looked for men who were continuing to be filled with the Holy Spirit and were growing in their walk with the Lord.

The apostles gave a great example for us to follow today. Apparently, they did not assume that everyone was continuing to grow in their walk with the Lord.

The phrase "full of the Spirit" is used in describing believers in the book of Acts.

It describes Stephen, the first martyr of the church:

> This proposal pleased the whole group. They chose Stephen, a man full of faith and of the Holy Spirit. (Acts 6:5)

It also describes Barnabas:

> He was a good man, full of the Holy Spirit and faith, and a great number of people were brought to the Lord. (Acts 11:22-24)

The phrase "full of the Spirit" expresses a continuing character development that enables people to minister in the

132

power of the Holy Spirit.

Believers who are full of the Spirit are empowered to lay aside their own desires so that they can be used in the fullness of the Spirit.

> For if you live according to the flesh, you will die; but if by the Spirit you put to death the misdeeds of the body, you will live. For those who are led by the Spirit of God are the children of God. (Romans 8:13-14)

God wants us to continue to maintain the ongoing work of the Holy Spirit in our lives so that in whatever situation we may face, we can rely upon the Holy Spirit to enable us to do what we may not be able to do on our own.

DAY 34

REMAINING FILLED WITH THE HOLY SPIRIT: PART 1

While they were worshiping the Lord and fasting, the Holy Spirit said, "Set apart for me Barnabas and Saul for the work to which I have called them." So after they had fasted and prayed, they placed their hands on them and sent them off. (Acts 13:2-3)

As we discuss the desire to continue to grow in our work with God and continue to experience the fullness of his Spirit, we must learn to adopt some regular practices in our lives. The first practice we must adopt is the regular practice of prayer.

In today's text, we see that Paul and Barnabas were fasting and praying. The early church would often choose to deny themselves food or other luxuries for a season in order to be more sensitive to the voice of God. They did this because Jesus modeled this. Many times, they fasted and prayed to gain greater revelation and wisdom concerning God's will, which was the case in today's text.

All throughout the book of Acts, you will see that believers committed themselves to regular times of prayer.

> They all joined together constantly in prayer, along with the women and Mary the mother of Jesus, and with his brothers.(Acts 1:14)

> They devoted themselves to the apostles' teaching and to the fellowship, to the breaking of bread and to prayer. (Acts 2:42)

One day Peter and John were going up to the temple at the time of prayer—at three in the afternoon. (Acts 3:1)

When they heard this, they raised their voices together in prayer to God. "Sovereign Lord," they said, "you made the heavens and the earth and the sea, and everything in them." (Acts 4:24)

We will give our attention to prayer and the ministry of the word. (Acts 6:4)

So Peter was kept in prison, but the church was earnestly praying to God for him. (Acts 12:5)

Many times, people will use the phrase "prayer helps us to win the battle," which is quite true. However, many times I have noticed that prayer actually is the battle.

Prayer doesn't change God—prayer changes us. The more we pray, the more we become like Jesus, and that is the ultimate purpose for being filled with the Holy Spirit.

DAY 35

REMAINING FILLED WITH THE
HOLY SPIRIT: PART 2

*After they had further proclaimed the word of the Lord and
testified about Jesus, Peter and John returned to Jerusalem,
preaching the gospel in many Samaritan villages. (Acts 8:25)*

Along with the daily practice of prayer, God also wants us to
develop the practice of sharing the gospel with others. God
fills us with his Holy Spirit so that we can overcome our
fear of rejection, criticism, and persecution. The Holy Spirit
wants to help us to be able to speak about Jesus and our
faith with boldness.

If this is something that you need help with, you are not so
different from the early church. They prayed for the same
help to overcome this fear.

> "Now, Lord, consider their threats and enable your
> servants to speak your word with great boldness.
> Stretch out your hand to heal and perform signs and
> wonders through the name of your holy servant Je-
> sus." After they prayed, the place where they were
> meeting was shaken. And they were all filled with the
> Holy Spirit and spoke the word of God boldly.
> (Acts 4:29-31)

God can overcome our weaknesses and help us to bypass
the limits in our personalities. The early church made it a
common practice to tell others near and far about what
Jesus had done for them.

With great power the apostles continued to testify to the resurrection of the Lord Jesus. And God's grace was so powerfully at work in them all. (Acts 4:33)

Then Philip began with that very passage of Scripture and told him the good news about Jesus. (Acts 8:35)

But the Lord said to Ananias, "Go! This man is my chosen instrument to proclaim my name to the Gentiles and their kings and to the people of Israel." (Acts 9:15)

So get up and go downstairs. Do not hesitate to go with them, for I have sent them. (Acts 10:20)

While they were worshiping the Lord and fasting, the Holy Spirit said, "Set apart for me Barnabas and Saul for the work to which I have called them." So after they had fasted and prayed, they placed their hands on them and sent them off. The two of them, sent on their way by the Holy Spirit, went down to Seleucia and sailed from here to Cyprus. (Acts 13:2-4)

When we choose to obey the voice of the Holy Spirit and let him overwhelm our fears with faith, we can be encouraged about his work on the inside of us. God gave us the Baptism of the Holy Spirit to help us overcome our fears, realizing that his power is stronger than our insecurities.

DAY 36

REMAINING FILLED WITH THE HOLY SPIRIT: PART 3

Do not get drunk on wine, which leads to debauchery. Instead, be filled with the Spirit, speaking to one another with psalms, hymns, and songs from the Spirit. Sing and make music from your heart to the Lord, always giving thanks to God the Father for everything, in the name of our Lord Jesus Christ.
(Ephesians 5:18-21)

One of the most overlooked details in our walk with God is the practice of worshipping him. God wants to speak to us and help us change our thinking.

The most common way that God wants to speak to us is through his Word. He wants us not only to come to church and listen to the teaching, but he wants us to study his Word on our own as well. We don't have to read for hours at a time, but God wants us to be consistent every day.

When we study God's Word, we become like God's Word—strong and stable. God's Word tells us what God is really like. If you think the Holy Spirit is leading you to do something, check it out in the Bible before you do it. Remember, God's Word and the Holy Spirit do not compete with each other—they complement each other.

As we sing, we sing songs that are about God and his Word. The songs that affect us the most are the ones that tell us who he is. Songs that are about God are directed toward God. They lift our spirits, encourage our hearts, and fill us with a new sense of awe of his power and his character.

DAY 37

INTERCESSION

Finally, be strong in the Lord and in his mighty power. Put on the full armor of God, so that you can take your stand against the devil's schemes. For our struggle is not against flesh and blood, but against the rulers, against the authorities, against the powers of this dark world and against the spiritual forces of evil in the heavenly realms. Therefore put on the full armor of God, so that when the day of evil comes, you may be able to stand your ground, and after you have done everything, to stand. Stand firm then, with the belt of truth buckled around your waist, with the breastplate of righteousness in place, and with your feet fitted with the readiness that comes from the gospel of peace. In addition to all this, take up the shield of faith, with which you can extinguish all the flaming arrows of the evil one. Take the helmet of salvation and the sword of the Spirit, which is the word of God. And pray in the Spirit on all occasions with all kinds of prayers and requests. With this in mind, be alert and always keep on praying for all the Lord's people. (Ephesians 6:10-18)

As the Holy Spirit increases your burden to pray, it is important to realize that not all prayer is the same. Prayer is not always fun; sometimes, it is a burden.

Today's text compares every Christian to the ancient Roman army and tells how we should protect and arm ourselves just as they did.

Every Roman soldier had the following:

1.) Belt
2.) Breastplate

3.) Special shoes (Roman soldiers wore cleats so they would always have firm footing.)
4.) Shield
5.) Helmet
6.) Sword
7.) Spear

Notice that our text does not mention the spear, but it does give one more word of instruction: "Pray in the Spirit on all occasions with all kinds of prayers and requests."

The spiritual spear that we have is the weapon of prayer and intercession.

Remember how numbers in the Hebrew language have special meaning? The number 6 represents the number of man and the number 7 represents completion.

God enables us by his Spirit to be able to be completely covered when we pray in the Spirit. It is the spear that we launch against the enemy.

DAY 38

THE ARSENAL OF PRAYER

And pray in the Spirit on all occasions with all kinds of prayers and requests. With this in mind, be alert and always keep on praying for all the Lord's people. (Ephesians 6:18)

God not only gave us the Sword of the Spirit with which to attack the enemy, but he also gave us the spear of intercession. Just like the Roman army had several different types of spears, we as Christians have an entire arsenal of prayer.

The Arsenal of Prayer:

1.) The Prayer of Commitment

This is where we cast our cares upon God instead of letting our worries get out of control.

2.) The Prayer of Agreement

This is where two people come together and agree with the Word of God in prayer.

Do two walk together unless they have agreed to do so? (Amos 3:3)

Again, truly I tell you that if two of you on earth agree about anything they ask for, it will be done for them by my Father in heaven. (Matthew 18:19)

But when you ask, you must believe and not doubt, because the one who doubts is like a wave of the sea, blown and tossed by the wind. (James 1:6)

And the prayer offered in faith will make the sick person well; the Lord will raise them up. If they have sinned, they will be forgiven. (James 5:15)

3.) The Prayer of Binding and Loosing

This is where we take our authority over the devil and speak faith and life into situations.

I will give you the keys of the kingdom of heaven; whatever you bind on earth will be bound in heaven, and whatever you loose on earth will be loosed in heaven. (Matthew 16:19)

4.) The Prayer of Worship

This is where we acknowledge God and his power in our life and in the earth. He has conquered and will conquer again.

5.) The Prayer of Thanksgiving

This is when we take time to recognize and thank God for all he has done in our life.

6.) The Prayer of Supplication

This is a type of prayer when we ask for specific things (wisdom, favor, blessings, etc.).

7.) Praying in the Spirit

Praying in the Spirit is the machine gun of prayers because

we are praying the entire arsenal of prayer at the same time.

God wants us to pray in our regular language (with the understanding) and in our prayer language (with our spirit) so that whatever situation we face, we know that we are covered.

DAY 39

WHAT THE FLESH PRODUCES

So I say, walk in the Spirit, and you will not gratify the desires of the flesh. For the flesh desires what is contrary to the Spirit, and the Spirit what is contrary to the flesh. They are in conflict with each other, so that you are not to do whatever you want. But if you are led by the Spirit, you are not under the law. The acts of the flesh are obvious: sexual immorality, impurity and debauchery; idolatry and witchcraft; hatred, discord, jealousy, fits of rage, selfish ambition, dissensions, factions and envy; drunkenness, orgies, and the like. I warn you, as I did before, that those who live like this will not inherit the kingdom of God. (Galatians 5:16-21)

Living a life that is led by the Spirit of God is a wonderful life, indeed. Many times, when people are beginning their walk with God, the common question is "How do I know if that is God talking to me or if it is just me wanting to do something out of my own selfish desires?"

Remember, it is easy to understand the voice of God because God's voice will always line up with his Word.

In our text today, we see what following selfish desires will produce. Our selfish or fleshly desires are the exact opposite of what our spiritual desires will be. Many times, we have to train our minds to act on the opposite of what we might want to do and make sure that it first is what God wants.

When the text talks about our sinful nature in verses 19-21, God is telling us that these sins are what grieves the Holy Spirit and that they will rob us of our effectiveness and praise. They will bring nothing but destruction to our life and our spirit. God's Spirit will never tell anyone to indulge in these activities, and his Spirit will not be active in anyone's life who does.

These are the behaviors of someone who is not filled with the Holy Spirit, not those of one who is Spirit-filled. What the flesh produces has natural consequences as well as spiritual consequences. It damages our spiritual life so much that our eternal life will be spent separate from God.

If what the flesh produces is so terrible, and the opposite of the flesh is the Spirit, then what the Spirit produces must be that much more powerful and enjoyable.

DAY 40

WHAT THE SPIRIT PRODUCES

But the fruit of the Spirit is love, joy, peace, forbearance, kindness, goodness, faithfulness, gentleness and self-control. Against such things there is no law. Those who belong to Christ Jesus have cruci-fied the flesh with its passions and desires. Since we live by the Spirit, let us keep in step with the Spirit. Let us not become conceited, provoking and envying each other. (Galatians 5:22-26)

In any health program, we are told what to avoid eating and what is good for our bodies. We should want to totally avoid everything that our selfish desires will produce. However, our text today shows us that anything the Spirit will produce, we can and should indulge in liberally. The fruit of the Spirit is an all-you-can-eat buffet. There is no limit.

We can often know whether or not something is good for us by looking at what it is producing. If we don't like what we are reaping in our lives, we need to change what we are planting.

Our flesh desires that which is opposite to what the Spirit desires, and the flesh will produce a harvest of things that will destroy our physical, spiritual, and eternal lives.

The things that the Spirit produces will produce a harvest that will strengthen and encourage our physical, spiritual, and eternal life. God's Spirit produces love, joy, peace, patience, kindness, goodness, faithfulness, gentleness, and self-control. All of these things only serve us and others better.

When we pray in the Spirit, we know that we are praying the perfect will of God, and then we choose to live the life that Christ taught.

This is the Spirit-filled life—searching, studying, and choosing to trust that God's ways are the best ways.

The Spirit-filled life has been better than I could begin to imagine. May you continue to grow in what you know and choose to be filled afresh and anew, every day.

ACKNOWLEDGEMENTS

It takes a great deal of help and encouragement to write a book, and I want to make sure that I thank those who were vital to it.

To my beautiful wife, Jennifer—from proofreading to grammar checking, this book is just as much yours as it is mine. I absolutely adore you.

To Mom and Dad—for encouraging me that I should do this and that I could do this.

To Randy Valimont—for being the most Pentecostal person I have ever known.

To Dr. Wave Nunnally—for being my theological accountability partner on this project and making sure that I "put in the work" to rightly divide the Word of Truth.

To my sisters Laura and Colleene—for cheering and clapping when I announced the book was done and sent to the editors.

To the Pastoral Staff, Board of Directors, Elders, Trustees and congregation of Coastal Church—for helping us to love where we live and being people who truly believe that "The Gulf Coast Will Be Saved."

Made in the USA
Middletown, DE
09 May 2021

38813386R00086